LOOKING FORWARD

Myeong-Hee Seong, Chase Karcher, Erika Choe

지식인

Authors

Myeong-Hee Seong
Ph.D. in English Education, Korea University
Professor, Eulji University

Chase Karcher
M.A. Cultural Studies, Kyung Hee University
Professor, Eulji University

Erika Choe
M.Ed. International Education, Framingham State University
Professor, Eulji University

Looking Forward

2022년 4월 20일 초판 1쇄 인쇄
2022년 4월 30일 초판 1쇄 발행

지은이 | Myeong-Hee Seong · Chase Karcher · Erika Choe
펴낸이 | 김종욱 · 명사동
펴낸곳 | 지식인
등 록 | 제301-2013-134호
주 소 | 서울시 도봉구 도봉로 180길 20 투웨니퍼스트 102동 602호
전 화 | 02)2266-8606
팩 스 | 02)2266-8607
E-mail | jisikin2013@naver.com
홈페이지 | www.jisikinbook.co.kr

ISBN 979-11-90815-95-6 (93740)

값 15,000원

Table of Contents

Looking Forward

Unit 1

Logging into Class

In this Unit...

Vocabulary	Grammar
in-person, hands-on, renowned, upsides, address, affordable, appealing, spotty	Gerunds and Infinitives
Reading Topic	**Speaking Skill**
Online Education	Having Deeper Conversations

Building Communication

to be honest, as a result of, used to ~

Preview

A. Conversation. *Read the conversation below.*

Brian Hey, Ashley. How are your classes going?

Ashley *To be honest,* online classes are tough. It's hard to focus sometimes. I'm easily distracted.

Brian Yeah, tell me about it. Don't you think classes are better in-person? I do.

Ashley Well, there are pros and cons. My major classes are hands-on, so it's difficult to learn online. Theory-based classes, like my English class, are easier because I can watch the lectures over and over.

Brian Good point. I guess I was only thinking about the downsides, not the upsides.

B. Warm-up. *Write 3 pros and 3 cons for taking classes online. Are online classes better than in-person classes?*

1. ____________	1. ____________
2. ____________	2. ____________
3. ____________	3. ____________

C. Write & Discuss. *Choose either online classes or in-person classes, then use your answers from above to argue for your side.*

____

____

____

Vocabulary Focus

A. Definition Matching. *Write the letter next to the correct word.*

_______ 1. in-person	A. not too expensive
_______ 2. hands-on	B. advantages, positive aspects
_______ 3. renowned	C. attractive to others
_______ 4. upsides	D. face-to-face
_______ 5. address	E. well known by many people
_______ 6. affordable	F. unreliable, inconsistent
_______ 7. appealing	G. direct experience
_______ 8. spotty	H. begin to solve an a problem

B. Fill in the Blanks. *Write the correct vocabulary word from above.*

1. Although the government made new laws, apartment prices still aren't _______________ in the Seoul area.
2. My phone isn't working. The connection seems to be a bit _______________ out here on the beach.
3. Sure, we all know that online learning has many problems, but we aren't considering the _______________.
4. Physical therapy can't be learned only in the classroom. It's a _______________ field; students need to practice with real people.
5. I got a job offer from a company in Gangnam. It's an _______________ offer, but I'm not sure it's right for me.
6. The professor has published more than 25 books and is highly _______________ in his field.
7. Although so much business is done online these days, I prefer to meet my clients and partners _______________.
8. Climate change is one of the major global issues of our time. If we continue to fail to _______________ it, the next generation will suffer.

Logging Into Class

Attending school looks a lot different than it used to just a few years ago. According to a 2019 report by the National Center for Education Statistics (NCES), nearly fifty-percent of students in 2017 were enrolled in at least some distance learning courses. This trend is only expected to continue. Therefore, it's important to look at both the upsides and downsides that it has on education.

Online schools are giving many people the opportunity to get an education that they might not have had before. Primary and secondary schools around the world are now joining long-time online schools like Khan Academy to provide education for anyone with an internet connection. Even renowned universities like Harvard, Stanford, and Yale offer free online courses, called MOOCs. This gives people around the world access to these courses. Additionally, online learning lets students study at their own speed and in the comfort of their home (or a hammock on the beach). Perhaps the most beneficial part of online learning is how affordable it is. These are all appealing aspects of digital learning.

However, researchers and educators are starting to feel the negative effects of online schooling on students' learning experience. Both teachers and students are struggling to adapt to this new way of learning and the changes it requires. It's not difficult to find reports of high absence rates due to technical problems, especially in schools with many low-income students, whose access to home computers and internet connections can be spotty. Another issue is that although students use technology in their daily lives, many do not know how to effectively use the tools at their disposal. Some students may notice that managing their time is more difficult online since they are not often reminded by teachers when to turn in their work. All of these things have an impact on students' learning.

Both educators and students are seeing many changes as a result of the growing need for online education. Despite its advantages, the perfect method for distance learning has yet to be found. One thing is for sure, online learning is not going anywhere anytime soon. If schools can address and fix these problems, the future of online education is bright.

Comprehension Check

A. Summary. *Fill each blank with information from the text.*

Online education is becoming more popular than before and it is expected to ______________. In 2017, almost ______________ of university students attended classes online, according to the NCES. Online education gives students the ______________ that they might not have had with face-to-face classes. For example, students have access to free online classes, called MOOCs, from ______________ universities such as Yale or Harvard. However, there are also negative ______________ of online education. One example is that many students do not know how to use technology ______________. If schools can ______________ the downsides, online education will have a bright future.

B. True/False. *If the sentence is false, correct it to make it true.*

1. In 2017, the majority of university students studied online. (T/F)
2. MOOCs are free online courses offered by schools. (T/F)
3. Online classes cost less than face-to-class classes. (T/F)
4. Fewer students are absent from online classes. (T/F)
5. Students know how to use online tools very well. (T/F)

C. Short Answer. *Answer each question with information from the text.*

1. According to the reading, what are some advantages of online learning?

____

____

____

2. What are some downsides to online education mentioned in the reading?

____

____

____

Building Communication

A. Learn. *Look at the phrases below to learn how to use them.*

1. To be honest - actually, speaking honestly

   A: *Let's eat tteokbokki for lunch!*

   B: *To be honest, I don't really like tteokbokki.*

2. as a result (of) - because of, due to

   As a result of the storm, all flights have been cancelled.

3. used to + (verb) - action done often in the past, not now

   I used to play badminton as a kid, but I haven't played in a long time.

B. Practice. *Complete the sentences with the phrases from above.*

1. My sister asked my opinion on her new haircut. I told her, ______________, it looks terrible. She was shocked.
2. Spicy food? I ______________ love it, but now it's too much for my stomach.
3. The government has announced new measures to reduce pollution, and ______________, many factories will reduce their operating hours.

C. More Practice. *Make sentences using the phrases above.*

1. to be honest

   ____

2. as a result of ~

   ____

3. used to ~

   ____

Grammar: Gerunds and Infinitives

Verbs that follow other verbs have to be changed to fit in a sentence.

Gerunds

A gerund is a verb that is used like a noun. It's made by adding +ing+to the end of verbs (i.e. "wimming").

Some verbs followed by gerunds include:

- keep
- enjoy
- finish
- delay
- avoid
- understand

*Infinitives**

An infinitive is a verb that can be used like a noun, adjective, or adverb. It's made by adding "to" the base form of the verb (i.e. "to swim").

Some verbs followed by infinitives include:

- plan
- hope
- decide
- need
- learn
- continue

* *There are special types of infinitives that are called* ***bare infinitives****. They are used after modals and certain verbs, such as "let", "made", "see/hear", "help", etc.*

A. Practice. ***Fill in the blank with the appropriate form of the verb.***

1. I learned __________ when I was five years old. (*swim*)
2. She said she hoped __________ them next weekend. (*see*)
3. My mom let me __________ to my friend's house last week. (*go*)
4. He was very upset and continued __________ all night. (*cry*)
5. Where's Rachel? I need __________ her something. (*ask*)

B. More Practice. ***With your group, write a short story below. Each sentence must contain either a gerund, verb, or bare infinitive.***

____

____

____

____

Speaking Skill: Having Deeper Conversations

Instead of talking about the weather or your hobbies, you might want to introduce a new topic, discuss a complex idea, share a personal issue or debate someone to change their mind. These deeper conversations require higher level speaking skills. These discussions broadly fall into 3 categories:

Informative: Explaining or sharing information

ex) *Sharing ideas, plans, new topics, lectures, etc.*

Persuasive: Trying to change someone's mind

ex) *Discussion, argument, debate, etc.*

Personal: Talking about personal or private issues

ex) *Dreams, worries, feelings, relationship issues, etc.*

You: Pizza is definitely better than tteokbokki.

Friend: Haha. That's a great joke.

You: It's no joke. I'm serious.

Friend: Have you lost your mind? Tteokbokki is the most classic and perfect food. The soft rice cake and warm, spicy sauce. I can taste it right now...

You: Wow, you really describe it well.
Suddenly, I want to eat tteokbokki...

A. Practice. *Answer the following questions.*

1. Read the above conversation. Which type of conversation is it?
2. What kind of details could you include to make this conversation more informative?
3. How could you include personal details to make this more persuasive?

B. More Practice. *Complete the following activities.*

1. What is a recent deep conversation you had with a friend? Discuss this topic with your team.
2. What is a unique opinion you have that is different from most people? Explain (*persuade*) your team why you think that way.

Wrap-Up

A. Write & Talk. ***Practice asking and answering the questions below to have a conversation with a partner or group.***

1. Have you ever had online classes? If so, which classes did you take?

   ____

   ____

2. Do you prefer taking classes in-person or online? Why?

   ____

   ____

3. What aspects of an online class make it a good or bad class (e.g. video audio quality, activity types, etc.)?

   ____

   ____

4. Is online education less valuable than traditional, face-to-face education?

   ____

   ____

5. What do you think school will look like in five years? Ten years?

   ____

   ____

B. Quiz. ***Take the quiz below to see how well you understood the unit.***

1. Apple MacBooks might be more ______________, but Windows laptops are much more ______________.

   a. hands-on, appealing   c. hands-on, respected

   b. respected, upsides   d. appealing, affordable

2. Distance learning is another way to refer to:

   a. face-to-face classes   c. online universities

   b. online education   d. primary and secondary education

3. Verbs that are used like nouns are called:

a. infinitives
b. bare infinitives
c. gerunds
d. conjunctions

4. ______________ the new policy, cell phones must be turned off during class.

a. To be honest
b. As a result of
c. Hands-on
d. Used to

5. Which type of deeper conversation describes explaining your favorite book to a friend?

a. informative
b. personal
c. persuasive
d. formal

Notes. ***Use the space below to take notes on this unit.***

Unit 2
Before It's Too Late

In this Unit...

Vocabulary	Grammar
severe, natural disaster, climate, acknowledge, atmosphere, take up, urge, sustainable	Active vs. Passive Voice
Reading Topic	**Speaking Skill**
Climate Change	Starting Conversations

Building Communication

according to, work toward(s), make a difference

Preview

A. Conversation. *Read the conversation below.*

Charlotte	The weather has been really crazy lately. There have been a lot of reports of natural disasters on the news.
Ariel	Yeah, that's true. I heard that it's because of climate change.
Charlotte	Really? We really need to start addressing it before it gets even worse.
Ariel	Speaking of climate change, it was discussed in our Environmental Science class last semester. Do you remember?
Charlotte	I vaguely remember the teacher saying that the situation was becoming severe... I didn't pay much attention in that class.

B. Warm-up. *Write 2 pros and 2 cons about each season. Are you a summer person or a winter person?*

	Summer	Winter
Pros	1. ________	1. ________
	2. ________	2. ________
Cons	1. ________	1. ________
	2. ________	2. ________

C. Write & Discuss. *What are your favorite activities to do during summer? In winter?*

____

____

____

Vocabulary Focus

A. Definition Matching. *Write the letter next to the correct word.*

_______ 1. severe	A. push something to happen
_______ 2. natural disaster	B. the air that covers the earth
_______ 3. climate	C. able to continue or be supported
_______ 4. acknowledge	D. an event in nature that causes a lot of damage, death, or injuries
_______ 5. atmosphere	E. admit that something is true
_______ 6. take up	F. very serious, harsh, or extreme
_______ 7. urge	G. begin or start doing
_______ 8. sustainable	H. typical weather in a certain region

B. Fill in the Blanks. *Write the correct vocabulary word from above.*

1. The couple realized that their lifestyle was not ________________ and they would need to start saving money for their future.
2. Gianna's boss was very ________________ to all the employees and they eventually quit to find better jobs where they'd be treated better.
3. The increasing pollution in the air is making Earth's ________________ harmful for humans to breathe.
4. A lot of people like to travel to tropical places like Hawaii or Guam for vacation because they have warmer ________________.
5. My mom always ________________ me to study so that I can get a job as a doctor, but I already told her I want to be an artist.
6. Pollution continues to increase every year which is causing horrible ________________, like typhoons and forest fires, to occur more frequently.
7. After seeing the results in person, the president of the company had to ________________ that there was a problem and start working to fix it.
8. While between jobs, Josephine ________________ a couple of new hobbies and learned some new skills.

Before It's Too Late

New articles about natural disasters like more severe hurricanes or record-breaking temperatures are written more each year. In the United States alone, the number of climate disasters recorded per year has continued to increase since the 1940s, with numbers especially high starting in the early 2000s. Similar situations are being reported for other regions around the world. The importance of climate change is something that all people must acknowledge if we ever hope to fix the problem.

In order to address the issue of climate change, the causes must be understood. *According to* NASA, the changes in our climate are due to the "greenhouse effect" This is when some gases in the atmosphere do not allow heat to escape from Earth. Gases such as carbon dioxide (CO2), methane, nitrous oxide, etc. are made as a result of human activities. These trapped gases raise the temperature of the planet which has different effects in different regions. For example, some places may see less rain while in others there may be more.

So what is being done now to fight climate change? In 2015, many countries joined together to create the Paris Agreement. Those countries that signed this treaty agreed to *work towards* reducing greenhouse gas pollution to prevent global temperatures from rising more by 2030. Unfortunately, the UN reported in 2018 that the targets are not being reached fast enough. This failure by governments around the world has caused some individuals to take up the fight, including children. In 2018, Greta Thunberg started to skip school to raise awareness about the climate change crisis. Her strike inspired many people around the world and she still fights today as a climate change activist.

The World Wide Fund (WWF) suggests people can do a lot to *make a difference*. This includes voting for politicians who will make policies to protect the earth, contacting brands and companies on social media to urge them to change how they make products, and reducing how much you buy. In addition, they also say people can live in a sustainable way by not eating a lot of animal products, travel by foot or bike when possible, and trying to make less trash by buying and using less plastic. Can you think of other ways that you can begin to make a difference starting today?

Comprehension Check

A. Summary. *Fill each blank with information from the text.*

Since the mid 1940s, ________________ have increased all over the world causing incredible damage and killing thousands of people. They are a result of ________________ which is caused by the "greenhouse effect" This is when ________________ that are trapped in the earth's air as a result of human activities. In order to try to stop climate change, countries around the world signed the ________________; however, the UN reported that as of 2018 they have not been successful. Organizations like the WWF are ________________ people to make changes like buying less and voting for politicians who will make policies to save the earth.

B. True/False. *If the sentence is false, correct it to make it true.*

1. Climate change is a problem that has grown in recent years. (T/F)
2. The increasing gases in Earth's atmosphere are a result of animal activities. (T/F)
3. The goals set by the Paris Agreement have been met in 2018. (T/F)
4. Greta Thunberg is a student who stopped going to school in order to begin fighting for climate change. (T/F)
5. There is nothing that we can do to stop climate change. (T/F)

C. Short Answer. *Answer each question with information from the text.*

1. In your own words, describe the "greenhouse effect"?

   ____

   ____

2. According to the reading, what are some ways that you can help to fight climate change in your daily life?

   ____

   ____

Building Communication

A. Learn. *Look at the phrases below to learn how to use them.*

1. according to (noun) - As said by

   According to recent news, the popularity of tablet computers is decreasing.

2. work toward(s) - make progress toward achieving

   Many countries are *working towards* reducing harmful greenhouse gases.

3. make a difference - have a strong effect (usually positive)

   Although eating organic food is expensive, it really does *make a difference* in your health.

B. Practice. *Complete the sentences with the phrases from above.*

1. Which phone is better? Apple? Samsung? Does it ________________ ?
2. A: There are many problems with public transportation.

   B: Yes, but the government is ________________ a solution.

3. ________________ my brother, who works in construction, the new city hall building will take about 3 years to finish.

C. More Practice. *Make sentences using the phrases above.*

1. according to ~

   ____

2. work towards ~

   ____

3. make a difference

   ____

Grammar: Active vs. Passive Voice

English speakers choose how to present the relationship between the subject, verb, and object (if one is present) by using either *active voice* or *passive voice.*

Active Voice

Active voice is when the subject of a sentence is also the actor and performs the verb's action. (*Most sentences are in active voice.*)

subject (actor) + verb + object (target)

→ My aunt visited her sister in the hospital yesterday.

Passive Voice

Passive voice is when the subject of the sentence is the target (receiver) of the verb's action. The focus is on the target. The actor may be unknown.

subject (target) + be-verb + verb p.p. (+ "by" actor)

→ These muffins were made by my mom.

A. Practice. ***Look at the sentences and decide whether they are written in active ("A") or passive voice ("P").***

1. The man was attacked by a random person. ______
2. Ashe had gotten a nice present from her friend. ______
3. She was bored at the party. ______
4. The monster attacked the town. ______
5. The president was escorted by his guard. ______
6. My keys were stolen yesterday. ______

B. More Practice. ***Change the active voice sentences into passive voice.***

1. Lisa has cleaned the windows.

   ____

2. They are serving lunch.

   ____

3. James will finish the work soon.

   ____

Speaking Skill: Starting Conversations

There are many ways to start a conversation. You can introduce a topic using a question, statement, or comment.

Question: Any question about the topic

Did you see the news?

Have you heard of Mark Manson?

What do you think about ________?

Statement: A direct statement about the topic

I heard that Lisa is getting married.

John didn't come to class yesterday.

My mom was attacked by a pigeon.

Comment: A comment on the current situation or surroundings

I really like your necklace.

The weather is so cold today.

I can't believe how expensive that bag is!

A. Practice. *Practice introducing each topic.*

1. Write a question to introduce: "Juhyun got a new job."

____

2. Write a statement to introduce a recent news story.

____

3. Write a comment to start a conversation about fashion.

____

B. Speaking Practice. *Introduce the following topics to your classmates using a question, statement, or comment.*

Movie	New cafe	Recent news
YouTuber	Good restaurant	New fashion
Appearance	TV show	Computer game

Wrap-Up

A. Write & Talk. ***Practice asking and answering the questions below to have a conversation with a partner or group.***

1. What are some effects of climate change that you have seen in your personal life?

   ____

   ____

2. What human activities do you know of that create some of the harmful gases mentioned in the reading? Do you do any of them?

   ____

   ____

3. What changes could you see yourself making in order to help protect the environment?

   ____

   ____

4. Do any of your friends do anything to help protect the environment? If so, what do they do? If not, could you try to convince them to start?

   ____

   ____

5. Do you think that it's possible to reverse the current effects of climate change? Why or why not?

   ____

   ____

B. Quiz. ***Take the quiz below to see how well you understood the unit.***

1. Scientists say that the increase in ____________ is due to ____________ change.

   a. urges, acknowledge
   c. severe, climate
   b. natural disasters, climate
   d. atmosphere, climate

2. When gases in the atmosphere prevent heat from escaping the planet it is called ________________.

a. the Paris Agreement
b. the World Wide Fund
c. a natural disaster
d. the greenhouse effect

3. Which sentence is correctly written in passive voice?

a. My niece was selected to go to her university of choice.
b. I was excited to go to the park with my friends.
c. Sherle was ask the answer to the question by her teacher.
d. There are many different ways to do the same thing.

4. Gi-hoon studies for class and works hard at his job because he is ________________ his dreams.

a. making a difference
b. working towards
c. used to
d. trying out

5. Which of the following is not a way to start a conversation?

a. questions
b. statements
c. stories
d. comments

Notes. ***Use the space below to take notes on this unit.***

Unit 3

Should I Stay or Should I Go?

In this Unit...

Vocabulary	Grammar
wanderlust, immerse, seek out, outbound, besides, thrilling, vibrant, landmark	Qualifiers
Reading Topic	**Speaking Skill**
Traveling: Abroad vs. Local	Supporting an Argument
Building Communication	
(be) itching to ~, a breath of fresh air, butterflies in one's stomach	

Preview

A. Conversation. *Read the conversation below.*

Lily I'm going to try going on a staycation this year.

Julian Why? If you have the chance, you should go abroad. It's much more fun. Plus, you can seek out new adventures.

Lily Yeah, it can be, but when I was a kid, my family didn't have a lot of money and couldn't travel abroad, so we did staycations. They were very fun. I also read in the Korea Times that due to the pandemic, over 90% of families are doing staycations.

Julian If that's the case, then I am pretty sure a lot of local places will have good deals. It could also be a nice chance to immerse yourself in your own local community.

Lily I hope so!

B. Warm-up. *Write 3 pros about traveling and 3 about staying home. Do you enjoy traveling? Or do you prefer to stay at home?*

1. ______________________	1. ______________________
2. ______________________	2. ______________________
3. ______________________	3. ______________________

C. Write & Discuss. *After writing pros for each, do you feel differently? Which type are you? Write 2-3 sentences.*

____

____

____

Vocabulary Focus

A. Definition Matching. *Write the letter next to the correct word.*

______	1. wanderlust	A. become deeply involved in
______	2. seek out	B. also, in addition
______	3. immerse	C. easily recognized object or place
______	4. outbound	D. strong desire to travel
______	5. besides	E. traveling away from a particular place
______	6. thrilling	F. search for, look for
______	7. landmark	G. bright, full of energy
______	8. vibrant	H. exciting

B. Fill in the Blanks. *Write the correct vocabulary word from above.*

1. When our favorite restaurant closed down, my friends and I had to ________________ a new place to have dinner on Friday nights.
2. People who love history often visit my hometown. There are a few local ________________ that were important during the Joseon era.
3. When I find a new author that I like, I totally ________________ myself in their work. I have to read all of their books!
4. My older sister really has a lot of ________________. She is always either traveling, or planning her next trip.
5. Did you see the new show on Netflix? It was so ________________! I couldn't stop watching!
6. Although COVID has decreased the amount of ________________ travelers, tourism is still a huge business around the world.
7. The rainforest in Malaysia is so ________________! All the colorful animals and plants make it seem like a magical place.
8. The Italian restaurant looks delicious, but it's a little too expensive. ________________, I'm not in the mood for pasta today.

Should I Stay or Should I Go?

Do you have a case of wanderlust? Are you just *itching to* travel? Don't worry, it's natural! Humans are a wandering species. Traveling has been a part of life since the ancient days of hunter-gatherers. Our ancestors traveled to find food, water, and better weather. Although traveling these days is much easier and more convenient than in the distant past, we still seek out the same things: warm weather, beautiful sights, and delicious food. New experiences are *a breath of fresh air* in our otherwise repetitive routines. This includes immersing ourselves in a different country, language, and culture.

Overseas trips have become increasingly popular for travelers. Lots of people love traveling overseas. The number of Korean outbound travelers has increased steadily year-over-year, from just over 7 million in 2003, to more than 28 million in 2019 Rising incomes, number of English speakers, and increased ease of overseas travel are all contributing factors in the rise of outbound tourism. Besides, it's exciting when you enter that international terminal at the airport, isn't it? Walking into the airport, suitcase in hand, fresh and ready to take off on a wild, new adventure; just thinking about it can give you *butterflies in your stomach!*

Although traveling overseas can be thrilling, we often forget about the special places that surround us in our daily lives. Local landmarks, sightseeing spots, and historical locations can reveal more about our own culture and history, which can make our daily lives more vibrant and interesting. What mysteries happened in your city? What famous battles were fought? What great love stories or tragedies occurred? Each street, alleyway, park or mountain holds its own secrets, waiting to be discovered. Why not get out of your comfort zone and explore your own city or country? After learning about the places around you, you just might see your mundane, daily life in a new light.

Regardless of where we choose to travel, there is always more to discover. Have you ever traveled overseas? Where did you go? What did you find? It's fun to explore faraway lands like the explorers of the past, but don't forget: you just might find something amazing in your own backyard. Go take a look! You can travel at home and abroad to get the best of both worlds!

Comprehension Check

A. Summary. ***Fill each blank with information from the text.***

Having a bit of ________________ is natural because humans are a ________________ species. In the past, humans traveled to find the necessities of life, such as food, water, and ________________. These days, we travel to immerse ourselves in new cultures and to give ourselves a break from our ________________ routines. Millions of people are taking trips in their own country, as well taking ________________ trips to foreign countries. Overseas travel can be exciting, but local trips within our own country can be surprising and fun as well. For example, you could learn some history online, then visit a local ________________ to see the real place! Wherever you choose to travel, you can find something amazing if you look for it.

B. True/False. ***If the sentence is false, correct it to make it true.***

1. Traveling has been a part of human life since tribal times. (T/F)
2. Korean outbound travelers increased by over 20 million in just 16 years. (T/F)
3. Local areas have nothing interesting to discover. (T/F)
4. Traveling in the past was much more convenient than now. (T/F)
5. Increasing incomes is one reason that travel has increased. (T/F)

C. Short Answer. ***Answer each question with information from the text.***

1. What are the reasons that overseas travels have increased every year?

____

____

2. What can we learn about by visiting local landmarks or locations?

____

____

Building Communication

A. Learn. *Look at the phrases below to learn how to use them.*

1. (be) itching to - really want to

   Ugh, I've been working all day. I'm itching to go home and watch my favorite drama!

2. a breath of fresh air - a new, welcome change

   A: *This place is great! I was tired of my boring routine.*

   B: *Me too! This trip is a breath of fresh air.*

3. butterflies in one's stomach - to feel nervous

   A: *Are you ready for your date?*

   B: *No! I have butterflies in my stomach!*

B. Practice. *Complete the sentences with the phrases from above.*

1. Even though my interview is next week, I'm nervous! I have __________ __________________ just thinking about it!
2. A: How was your vacation?

   B: Fantastic! It was ____________________________.
3. I was on vacation with my family, so I haven't been able to play my online game. I'm ____________________________ get home and play!

C. More Practice. *Make sentences using the phrases above.*

1. be itching to ~

   ____
2. a breath of fresh air

   ____
3. butterflies in one's stomach

   ____

Grammar: Qualifiers

Qualifiers are descriptive words that come before adjectives or adverbs and modify their meaning, by limiting or enhancing them.

← Weaker	Average	Stronger →
• *not very/really*	• *quite*	• *so/very/really*
• *kind of*	• *fairly*	• *extremely*
• *a bit*	• *pretty*	• *incredibly*
• *a little*	• *somewhat*	• *super*

→ It was a little difficult to hear the teacher because class was noisy.

The qualifiers above cannot be used with comparatives/superlatives. Instead, use the ones below:

Comparatives	Superlatives
• *much*	• *definitely*
• *a lot*	• *by far*
• *far*	• *far and away*

→ Elephants are much bigger than I imagined they were.

A. Practice. ***Complete the sentences with a qualifier that best fits.***

1. I think I failed the exam. It was ______________ easy at all.
2. The airport was ______________ the busiest that I've ever seen it.
3. The weather this summer was ______________ hot. The news said that it was dangerous to be outside for too long.
4. The problem is ______________ worse than he described. We will need a lot more time to fix the computer.
5. I'm going to be ______________ late, around five minutes. I apologize in advance.

B. More Practice. ***Write a sentence for each of the pairs of words below. Make sure to use one of the qualifiers from above.***

1. (Maratang/spicy) ______________________________________
2. (Learning English/difficult) ______________________________
3. (Korea's public transportation system/convenient) ______________

Speaking Skill: Supporting an Argument

Your "argument" is your opinion, your main point or your side in a conversation. You can make your opinions and ideas stronger with support. Depending on the topic, you can support your argument in various ways:

Reasons: Simple, but powerful
We should take the bus because it's faster.

Examples: An example case that supports your argument
For example, ...

Data & Statistics: Exact numbers from research about the topic
According to MBC News, 60% of people...

Expert Opinion: Quote from an expert in the topic
Professor Park at SNU said "These days..."

Anecdote: Short personal story to connect with audience
When I was in high school, .../ In my case, ...

A. Practice. ***Search online for support for the following two arguments. Write 1-2 sentences using the research you found.***

1. Bullying is a major social issue in middle and high schools.

____

____

2. Sleep is an essential part of our health.

____

____

B. More Practice. ***Debate the following topics with your team using any type of support.***

Americano vs. Cafe Latte

HomePlus vs. Emart

Drinking alcohol has benefits

Neo is the best Kakao character

Wrap-Up

A. Write & Talk. ***Practice asking and answering the questions below to have a conversation with a partner or group.***

1. Which foreign countries have you traveled to? Which would you like to visit in the future?

____

____

2. Search for and write about an interesting historical place in your town. Would you like to visit? Why or why not?

____

____

3. Do you feel wanderlust? Or are you fine without travel? In your opinion, why are people different in this way?

____

____

4. When you travel, what kinds of places or activities do you seek out?

____

____

5. The reading mentions your "comfort zone". What is your personal comfort zone? What do you want to try that you haven't yet?

____

____

B. Quiz. ***Take the quiz below to see how well you understood the unit.***

1. I got lost when I was on my way to a new place when travelling until I found the ______________ that a local told me to look for.

   a. wanderlust c. vibrant

   b. landmark d. outbound

2. Traveling to other countries is exciting, but just as exciting is traveling to ______________.

a. the sea
b. places I already know
c. the mountains
d. local places

3. Genie hates giving presentations because she always has ______________.

a. a breath of fresh air
b. the best of both worlds
c. butterflies in her stomach
d. making a difference

4. A lot of people visited the restaurant to do the ramen eating challenge, but a lot of people failed because it was ______________ spicy. Many people who ate it were sweating and even crying!

a. not very
b. somewhat
c. extremely
d. by far

5. The following is what type of support? According to Cho Min-kyung, a researcher from the KCDC, wearing masks helps reduce the spread of many different types of diseases.

a. expert opinion
b. reasons
c. example
d. data and statistics

Notes. ***Use the space below to take notes on this unit.***

Unit 4

Rolling out of Bed and into Work

In this Unit...

Vocabulary	Grammar
telework, take off, remote, look at, alternative, income, nontraditional, outbreak	Tag Questions
Reading Topic	**Speaking Skill**
Remote Work	Clarifying and Paraphrasing

Building Communication
from time to time, change of pace, worth it

Preview

A. Conversation. *Read the conversation below.*

Lauren	My girlfriend has been working remotely recently. Your boyfriend is working at home nowadays, isn't he?
Stacey	Yeah, he is. He's so annoying. He just horses around half the time.
Lauren	Sorry, what do you mean?
Stacey	Oh, I mean that he doesn't focus on his work well and plays games on his phone or naps when he isn't busy.
Lauren	Yeah, Sarah does that, too. Everyone does that, don't they?
Stacey	I guess so, but that's definitely a drawback of teleworking.

B. Warm-up. *How do you prefer to work? Circle all of your answers.*

Do you work best with plenty of time? Or under pressure?

In a quiet place or a crowded place? In a team or alone?

Plenty of time	Under pressure
Quiet place	Crowded place
In a team	Alone

C. Write & Discuss. *Explain why you work best that way.*

____

____

____

Vocabulary Focus

A. Definition Matching. *Write the letter next to the correct word.*

______	1. telework	A. a possible or different option
______	2. take off	B. not typical, a new method of thinking or behaving
______	3. remote	C. consider or examine
______	4. look at	D. sudden increase or occurrence
______	5. alternative	E. start becoming popular or widespread
______	6. income	F. far away, from a distance
______	7. nontraditional	G. work outside of the office
______	8. outbreak	H. money that one receives from one's job

B. Fill in the Blanks. *Write the correct vocabulary word from above.*

1. The dentist ______________ Shelly's teeth and told her that she will need to have her wisdom teeth removed.
2. Many people in the older generation like to celebrate holidays the way they always have, but younger people are starting to celebrate in __________ ways.
3. Hee-jun had a good job that gave him a high ______________ but he always spent a lot every month, so he doesn't have any savings.
4. Leila was really excited when her hard work started to pay off and her small business really ______________.
5. The ______________ of the new disease created a lot of worry and disrupted the lives of all countries that were affected.
6. She really didn't like the new house because it was in a really ______________ location and not close to the city at all.
7. The company had to look at a(n) ______________ solution to make money when their current plan didn't work out.
8. Nowadays, it's common for employees to ______________ from home or in a cafe by their house instead of going to the company building.

Rolling out of Bed and into Work

When you see yourself going to work, you imagine wearing a suit or nice dress, don't you? However, in the future, more people may be wearing pajamas or no pants at all! In the 1970s, the idea of teleworking began but it really started to take off in the 2010s when technology became more advanced. In 2020, the spread of COVID-19 all over the world made remote work necessary. Since more companies have experience with remote work, researchers are starting to examine the effects.

The Pew Research Center looked at how working from home during the 21st century pandemic had affected American workers. For those whose jobs could be done at home, over half of workers said they would like to continue working from home after the outbreak ended. Meetings had also changed for the better. Over 60% of workers said that using online tools to meet coworkers was a good alternative to meeting face-to-face. A lot of workers were also more productive. Many workers, especially older workers, said that they are more easily motivated to do their work in this new setting. A majority also stated that it was easier to get their work done on time.

Although working from home has its benefits, it's not great for everyone. Workers' home life affected their productivity. Parents, especially mothers, struggled to get their work done without interruptions and maintain a good work-life balance. Workers' ability to do their job was affected by their income level. Many lower income workers stated that their jobs could not be done from home and if they could, they were still required to come into the office *from time to time*. Age also had an influence on workers. Younger workers reported having more difficulty working from home. They found it more difficult to meet deadlines, have the proper space or equipment to work, and feel motivated.

Although some people enjoyed the *change of pace*, not everyone is satisfied with working from home; moreover, others are predicting that how we work will be changed forever now that more companies have experience with this nontraditional way of working. It is impossible to tell if working remotely will continue to be a trend in the future, but it is *worth it* for companies and people to weigh both the good and the bad.

Comprehension Check

A. Summary. *Fill each blank with information from the text.*

Working from home began in the 1970s but became more popular over forty years later thanks to the improvements in ________________ that made it easier. The Pew Research Center looked into the effects of ________________ work and found that there are both good and bad aspects. A majority of workers said they preferred meeting coworkers ________________ as opposed to face-to-face and that it was easier to complete their work ________________. On the other side, many people, especially ________________, said it was difficult to do their work without ________________. Additionally, ________________ people said it was easier to meet deadlines and feel motivated when working from home. Regardless of how you feel about teleworking, it may be here to stay.

B. True/False. *If the sentence is false, correct it to make it true.*

1. Teleworking first became popular in the 1970s. (T/F)
2. Over 50% of workers reported enjoying working from home. (T/F)
3. Working from home reduces productivity and is not equally accessible to everyone. (T/F)
4. It's easier for younger people to work at home. (T/F)
5. Teleworking will definitely continue in the future. (T/F)

C. Short Answer. *Answer each question with information from the text.*

1. What are some of the benefits of working from home from the reading?

____

____

2. Who struggles the most to complete their work without interruption?

____

____

Building Communication

A. Learn. *Look at the phrases below to learn how to use them.*

1. from time to time - sometimes

   A: *Have you heard of Tom's Noodle stand near school?*

   B: *Of course! I have lunch there from time to time.*

2. change of pace - change from normal routine

   A: *Do you like your new job?*

   B: *Yeah! It's a nice change of pace from my old job.*

3. worth it - enjoyable or valuable even though it's hard work

   We had to wake up at 4:00am to hike Hallasan to see the sunrise, but it was totally worth it!

B. Practice. *Complete the sentences with the phrases from above.*

1. I used to visit my grandmother every weekend. But these days, I only see her ____________________.

2. A: Wow! You passed the licensure exam with a perfect score?

   B: Yes, well... I sacrificed all my free time, but I think it was

   ____________________.

3. Moving to Washington, D.C. was a big ____________________. I had to change my whole routine!

C. More Practice. *Make sentences using the phrases above.*

1. from time to time

   ____

2. change of pace

   ____

3. worth it

   ____

Grammar: Tag Questions

Tag questions are short questions added to the end of regular sentences to elicit a response or confirm information.

They are made by adding an *auxiliary verb** and a *subject pronoun*.

Be verb	Regular verb	Auxiliary Verb
→ Use be verb	→ Use do	→ Use same aux. verb
Susy and Jean are sisters, aren't they?	You have an iPhone, don't you?	Sean has been there, hasn't he?

* If the verb in the main sentence is positive, the auxiliary verb in the tag question should be negative. If it is negative, then the auxiliary verb is positive.

→ Kyle went to the party, didn't he? (*pos. verb/neg. tag*)

→ She doesn't like sweet food, does she? (*neg. verb/pos. tag*)

A. Practice. *Add a tag question to the following sentences.*

1. They live in London, ______________?
2. They have been to Japan, ______________?
3. Lauren will come at six, ______________?
4. He can't help, ______________?
5. Joanne wasn't home today, ______________?

B. More Practice. *Look at the conversation below and add a tag question where needed. If no tag question is needed, write "X".*

Anna	We're all going to see a movie this weekend	____________
Robin	Henry is going, too	____________
Anna	Yeah. Is that a problem	____________
Robin	Kind of...	____________
Anna	Why	____________
Robin	We had a fight. You knew about that	____________
Anna	No, I had no idea	____________

Speaking Skill: Clarifying & Paraphrasing

If you don't understand something in English, you can ask for clarification (clarify [v.]: *to make clear*). You can ask for clarification when confused or you need more information. You can give clarification when others ask you.

Asking for clarification: (1) Get attention, (2) Ask

Get attention	Ask
Excuse me.	Can you repeat that? / Can you say that again?
I'm sorry.	Could you explain? / Can you give me an example?

Giving clarification: (1) Acknowledge, (2) Repeat or Explain

Acknowledge	Repeat or Explain
Yes. / Of course.	I said (that)... / I mean... / In other words,
Sure. / Sorry.	What I mean is

You can use paraphrasing to give clarification. Paraphrasing is repeating information in a simpler and clearer way.

A. Practice. *Write an appropriate clarification phrase.*

Justin	We have to complete the project by today, don't we?
Lisa	________________________________? I didn't hear you.
Justin	________________________we have to finish the project ASAP.
Erin	The weather forecast calls for heavy precipitation tonight.
Jason	________________________________? I don't understand.
Erin	________________________________ it will rain later today.

B. More Practice. *Ask your classmates about the following topics, then use clarification phrases to ask for more information.*

Do you prefer spicy food? What type of TV shows do you like?

How do you like to spend your weekend?

Wrap-Up

A. Write & Talk. ***Practice asking and answering the questions below to have a conversation with a partner or group.***

1. Do you have experience working (or studying) from home? If so, how was it?

   ____

   ____

2. What are some of the advantages of working from home? What are some disadvantages?

   ____

   ____

3. What are some ways you could improve the disadvantages of working from home?

   ____

   ____

4. Do you think that teleworking is better for employers or employees? Why?

   ____

   ____

5. Would you prefer to telecommute to work or to work in an office full time? Why?

   ____

   ____

B. Quiz. ***Take the quiz below to see how well you understood the unit.***

1. Hugh was considering changing to a(n) _________ kind of job, but then his career really started to _________.

   a. alternative, take off
   b. nontraditional, take off
   c. alternative, telework
   d. outbreak, look at

2. When working remotely, many people prefer to do things online, such as _______ but others have difficulty with things like _________.

   a. productivity, emails
   c. meeting deadlines, equipment

b. travelling, being on time | d. meetings, work-life balance

3. Complete the sentence with the correct tag question: You haven't been to Chicago before, ________?

   a. did you
   c. had you
   b. didn't you
   d. haven't you

4. Michelle is an amazing figure skater. She said that she had to work extremely hard but it was ________.

   a. a change of pace
   c. the best of both worlds
   b. worth it
   d. a breath of fresh air

5. What best completes the conversation below?

   A: I really had an epiphany and so I became vegan.

   B: I'm sorry, could you explain that to me? I don't quite understand.

   A: ________________________________

   a. Sure. I said, "I really had an epiphany and so I became vegan."
   b. Of course, in other words I realized something so I changed my lifestyle and became vegan.
   c. It's okay.

Notes. ***Use the space below to take notes on this unit.***

Unit 5

All Work and No Play

In this Unit...

Vocabulary	Grammar
norms, burnout, R&R, irritability, reevaluate, priority, neglect, follow through	Present/Future Progressive
Reading Topic	**Speaking Skill**
Work-Life Balance	Reported Speech

Building Communication

take precedence over, on the other hand, before you know it

Preview

A. Conversation. *Read the conversation below.*

Luis I heard that you're going to the mountains this weekend.

Serena Yeah, I'll be going on Saturday. I always try to get a little R&R on the weekends. Won't you be working this weekend?

Luis Yeah. I'll be working all weekend. We have a deadline soon so my boss said that we need to work. I'm starting to feel the burnout.

Serena I read that is a big problem. According to the news, 40% of workers reported having to work overtime in the last six months.

Luis Do you know if you have to work overtime?

Serena I don't. I am really lucky I have a good work-life balance. It's definitely not the norm.

B. Warm-up. *Write three activities you do when avoiding your work.*

Some people don't have balance because they work too much, while others play too much. What do you do when you're avoiding your work? How do you procrastinate?

1. ______________________________
2. ______________________________
3. ______________________________

C. Write & Discuss. *What advice would you give yourself to stop procrastinating and do your work on time?*

____

____

____

Vocabulary Focus

A. Definition Matching. *Write the letter next to the correct word.*

______	1. norms	A. continue action until it's completed
______	2. burnout	B. feeling annoyed
______	3. R&R	C. important things
______	4. irritability	D. usual, standard or expected social behavior
______	5. reevaluate	E. physically and mentally tired due to stress
______	6. priority	F. rest and relaxation
______	7. neglect	G. think again carefully or differently
______	8. follow through	H. not care for something well

B. Fill in the Blanks. *Write the correct vocabulary word from above.*

1. When I don't sleep well, I tend to ______________ my health. I'm lazy and eat junk food instead of eating well and exercising.
2. The final exam period was so tough. I studied all day for three weeks straight! I really need some ______________.
3. The rising cost of living is an issue for people around the world. Each government has to constantly ______________ it's laws and rules so their citizens can be healthy and productive.
4. As time goes on, social ______________ are always changing. 20 years ago no one had cell phones, but now they are central to our lives!
5. ______________ is a serious problem among medical workers. Long hours working with sick people can be tough, so take care of yourself!
6. If your life feels unbalanced, you might want to check your personal ______________. Where are you spending your time and energy?
7. We all have big dreams in life, but few people ______________.
8. Another symptom of stress is ______________. If you're feeling annoyed and anxious too often, it's time to make a change.

All Work and No Play

Work and life; these days, it's hard to separate the two. A constantly changing economy and rising cost of living has made our daily lives stressful and competitive. But we need time to relax and have a life, right? It's easy to let work *take precedence over* our personal lives; however, We do so at our own risk. Striking the right work-life balance is an essentical part of a healthy life. While achieving this balance partly depends on shifting cultural norms, there are plenty of changes we can make to our personal habits as well.

The norms and expectations of a society are a major factor in citizens' work-life balance. One sign of this balance, vacation time utilization, varies greatly across the world. The French, for example, have a greater number of vacation days available, and tend to use more of them. Japan, *on the other hand*, both receives and uses the fewest number of vacation days. Korea finds itself stuck in the middle. Government labor law requires a fair number of paid vacation time (15 days). However, due to social pressure, Koreans only use an average of 8.6 days per year. While recent trends seem to be changing, Korea remains a competitive environment.

What does an unhealthy work-life balance look like on a personal level? A good way to know is if you have symptoms of burnout: fatigue, insomnia, irritability, frequent sickness, etc. If that's the case, you need to take a day off and get some R&R. But if the issue continues, you need to dig deeper. How can we strike the right balance between work and play? First, you can try to reevaluate your priorities. Are you neglecting your health? Relationships? Your studies? If you're having trouble finding time, try making a schedule. Be strict with your personal time. Don't only think in terms of vacations, but also evenings and weekends. If you plan ahead and use your time wisely, you'll have more free time *before you know it*! Making a schedule and following through is a good way to achieve balance.

Work-life balance is an important part of a healthy life. Take a step back, reevaluate your priorities, and stick to a healthy schedule that works for you.

Comprehension Check

A. Summary. *Fill each blank with information from the text.*

A shifting economy and rising prices have made life more stressful and ________________. Finding the right balance between work and personal life can be tough, but it's important for a healthy life. On the social level, work-life balance can be measured by vacation time ________________. In Korea, the government labor law requires 15 vacation days, but some people do not use all of them due to social ________________. We can all make some personal changes as well. Try to avoid burnout, which can appear as fatigue, insomnia, and frequent ________________. If that's the case, get some rest. Also, you can reevaluate your ________________. Think carefully about how you spend your time and energy, and try to do more things that make you happy.

B. True/False. *If the sentence is false, correct it to make it true.*

1. A good work-life balance depends on social and cultural norms as well as personal habits. (T/F)
2. Japan uses more vacation time than France. (T/F)
3. Frequent sickness is a symptom of burnout. (T/F)
4. Korean labor law requires 8.6 vacation days per year. (T/F)
5. Making a schedule can create a healthy work-life balance. (T/F)

C. Short Answer. *Answer each question with information from the text.*

1. Why do people not use all of their vacation days?

____

____

2. What are some signs of burnout?

____

____

Building Communication

A. Learn. *Look at the phrases below to learn how to use them.*

1. take precedence over - to be more important than
   I have 7 midterm exams to study for, but my English exam is first. So that takes precedence over the others.
2. on the other hand - to give a different opinion or option
   Barbeque sounds great for dinner! On the other hand, I could really eat some pizza right now...
3. before you know it - very quickly, faster than expected
   The flight to Jeju is very short. You'll be there before you know it!

B. Practice. *Complete the sentences with the phrases from above.*

1. If you eliminate sugar from your food and start an exercise program, you'll lose weight and feel better ______________________!
2. We shouldn't let work ______________________ our personal lives. We need to find a balance.
3. I think living in the city is great. Access to everything you need and want. ______________________, living in the countryside would be nice, too, because you're surrounded by nature.

C. More Practice. *Make sentences using the phrases above.*

1. take precedence over ~
   ____
2. on the other hand
   ____
3. before you know it
   ____

Grammar: Present/Future Progressive

Present Progressive tense is used to describe an ongoing action in the present. It can also be used to talk about future plans that are already decided and sure to happen. It can be used with both stative and action verbs.

Subject	be-verb	v+ing	
Jamie	***is***	***studying***	*at E. University next fall.*
Jon and Kim	***are***	***playing***	*soccer at school right now.*

Future Progressive tense is used to describe an action that is expected to happen in the future and continue for a limited period of time. It can only be used with action verbs. (Use simple future with stative verbs.)

Subject	***will***	***be***	***v+ing***	
We	***will***	***be***	***watching***	*a movie tomorrow afternoon.*
Mi-jeong	***won't***	***be***	***working***	*next Saturday, so she can come.*

A. Practice. ***Complete the sentence below with the sentences with the correct form of the verb in parentheses.***

1. Mila ______________ (*learning*) how to play piano still, so she can't play really difficult songs yet.
2. I am busy at that time so I cannot attend the meeting. Tomorrow afternoon I ______________ (*take*) an exam.
3. Currently, I ___________ (*work*) at a convenient store, but I hope that by next year, I ______________ (*work*) at a good company.

B. More Practice. ***Write your future career plans. Be sure to include both the present and future progressive tenses.***

____

____

____

____

Speaking Skill: Reported Speech (Formal)

Certain verbs and phrases can be used to report the speech of others. You can report speech *directly or indirectly*. Formal reported speech is common when discussing news or research.

Source: Professor Lee Speech: "More than 40% of people support these rules."

Direct (exact words)	Professor Lee stated, "More than 40% of people support these rules."
Indirect (paraphrase)	According to Professor Lee, support for these new rules is upwards of 40%.

Phrases	Verbs (+ that)
According to __________,	reported, claimed, stated,
As reported by __________,	insisted, noted, argued, explained, confirmed,
	denied, advised, warned, cautioned

A. Practice. *Report the speech directly using a phrase or verb.*

1. Source: Oxford University Speech: "40% of students get insufficient sleep.

____

2. Source: recent research, Speech: "The rate of climate change is increasing every year."

____

B. More Practice. *Report the speech indirectly using verbs.*

1. Source: Dr. Roberts Speech: "Cleaning products are harmful to our health."

____

2. Source: NY Foundation, Speech: "New Yorkers are spending more money on transportation."

____

Wrap-Up

A. Write & Talk. ***Practice asking and answering the questions below to have a conversation with a partner or group.***

1. What is your favorite way to get some R&R?

   ____

   ____

2. What is one thing you could change to make yourself happier?

   ____

   ____

3. When was the last time you felt you didn't have a good balance between work and life? Looking back, how could you have prevented this issue?

   ____

   ____

4. Think about your priorities. Everyone has 24 hours each day. What do you spend most of your time doing? Write your top 3. Be honest.

   ____

   ____

5. Think about your answer to question 4. Are you satisfied with the top 3 things you spend time on? What would you change?

   ____

   ____

B. Quiz. ***Take the quiz below to see how well you understood the unit.***

1. Kimiko is difficult to be around lately because of her ____________, so her friends think she is suffering from ____________ at her job.

   a. burnout, priorities
   c. following through, priorities
   b. norms, R&R
   d. irritability, burnout

2. If having a good work-life balance is going to become standard, there needs to be a change in ___________ norms.

a. financial
b. social
c. personal
d. familial

3. Which of the following sentences is grammatically correct?

a. Let's find out when the next showing of the moving is or not.
b. Could you tell me whether free parking?
c. I wonder if she's coming to school today or not.
d. Do you think if when the concert starts tonight?

4. Working from home is really convenient. ___________, there are new problems like being easily distracted or not having the right equipment.

a. On the other hand
b. According to
c. In terms of
d. Before you know it

5. The following is an example of what type of reported speech: "As reported by the CDC, the outbreak was quickly contained."

a. Direct
b. Indirect

Notes. ***Use the space below to take notes on this unit.***

Unit 6
Getting Around

In this Unit...

Vocabulary	Grammar
pollution, consider, drastically, affordable, emit, encourage, go about, impact	Modals of Probability
Reading Topic	**Speaking Skill**
Modern Transportation	Alternative Perspectives
Building Communication	
cut from the same cloth, whereas, depending on	

Preview

A. Conversation. *Read the conversation below.*

Sofia You're going to the festival this weekend, aren't you?

Trevor Yeah, I am. Oh, speaking of the festival, how are you getting there? Are you considering driving your car there?

Sofia Yeah, I am, but I think I might take the subway.

Trevor Why? If I had a car, I'd never take the subway again.

Sofia Even though driving is convenient and may save time, it's not as good for the environment as taking public transport.

Trevor Environmentalists do argue that we should avoid driving because cars emit a lot of pollution; however; alternative modes of transport aren't always available. For example, public transport doesn't go to the countryside.

B. Warm-up. *Write three "pet peeves" you have about using public transportation.*

People spend hours everyday on public transportation. What are some things others do that annoy you on the bus or train?

1. ______________________________
2. ______________________________
3. ______________________________

C. Write & Discuss. *If you didn't have your phone, how would you pass the time on the bus or train? Write and share your answer.*

____

____

____

Vocabulary Focus

A. Definition Matching. *Write the letter next to the correct word.*

______	1. pollution	A.	an effect on; to have an effect on
______	2. consider	B.	push or help to action
______	3. drastically	C.	discharge or release
______	4. affordable	D.	harmful wastes found in the air, water, etc.
______	5. emit	E.	actively do something; busy yourself
______	6. encourage	F.	think about in a careful manner
______	7. go about	G.	be able to pay the price of something
______	8. impact	H.	to an extreme degree

B. Fill in the Blanks. *Write the correct vocabulary word from above.*

1. The young woman carefully ________________ which school she would attend because she only had one chance to go to school.
2. Young people have to always look for the most ________________ option when shopping because they do not have a lot of money to buy very costly items.
3. Killian took his car to the mechanic because it suddenly started to ________________ a strange smoke from the engine.
4. People often think that they can't ________________ climate change by making changes to their daily lives, but that is simply not true. It helps.
5. The mother was shocked by her child's sudden change in behavior, especially how he ________________ improved his grades from almost failing to the top of his class.
6. Since Zeon had some extra time, he decided to finally ________________ finishing the book he started last month.
7. Scientists warn that if humans do not begin to reduce the amount of ________________ made by human activity on the earth soon, then it will be too late to save the planet.
8. Sharla always ________________ her little sister to try her best, even when she doesn't feel like she can.

Getting Around

Nowadays, people have a lot of options when they want to travel from one place to another. However, modern transportation methods are not all *cut from the same cloth*. Some are faster and more convenient, *whereas* some produce a lot of pollution and use a lot of energy. These are things that people must consider when they choose how they travel around because they have real effects on our planet.

Compared to only a hundred years ago, the options for getting around have drastically increased, especially with public transportation. Taxis are common in many large cities but are harder to find outside cities in some countries. The cost is also very different *depending on* the country. In India or China, they are affordable, but in other countries like the United States, they can be costly. Buses are another option. Some cities have nice, large buses with advanced technology while others are very small and simply designed. Subways are common in many developed countries with very complex underground systems, but they cannot be found in a lot of poorer countries or far from the city. Although the number of private transportation options like cars, bikes, scooters, or walking hasn't changed much, technology and environmental needs have changed what these look like today and will look like in the future.

A critical issue that all countries are dealing with is climate change. One major reason for the rising global temperatures are the greenhouse gases (GHG) emitted by transportation. Twenty-eight percent of the United States's GHG emissions and over 17% of Australia's came from transportation. As a result, countries around the world are developing new ways to improve transportation. Countries are encouraging people to drive hybrid or electric cars instead of diesel cars. More ride-sharing services, like *Uber* or *Lyft*, are being offered to reduce the number of cars on the road in places where public transportation is not available. In places like South Korea, services for easily renting electric scooters and bikes are becoming more and more common.

As we go about our daily lives, people often only consider what is most convenient when they travel. However, thinking about the impact that our choice makes on the environment is equally as important. How will you get around when you step out of your house?

Comprehension Check

A. Summary. ***Fill each blank with information from the text.***

Compared to the past, there are more ________________ for travelling around. While some transportation methods are positive, some have negative effects on the planet, like creating a lot of ________________. Public transportation, like busses, taxis, and subways, have increased in many countries. Additionally, personal transportation methods have also changed due to technology and environmental needs. Transportation creates a lot of ________________ gases, so many countries are ________________ people to drive ________________ or electric cars, use ________________ services like Uber, or rent ________________ scooters in order to reduce pollution.

B. True/False. ***If the sentence is false, correct it to make it true.***

1. Some forms of transportation are harmful to the planet. (T/F)
2. Public transportation is well developed in all parts of the world. (T/F)
3. Due to the development of technology and the need to protect the planet, private transportation has changed in recent years. (T/F)
4. Gases created by transportation methods have a negative impact on global warming and climate change. (T/F)
5. Governments are encouraging people to drive more diesel cars to help reduce pollution. (T/F)

C. Short Answer. ***Answer each question with information from the text.***

1. Where does a large percentage of greenhouse gas pollution come from in bigger countries like the United States and Australia?

   ____

   ____

2. What are some ways that countries/companies/people are changing how they get around in order to reduce pollution?

   ____

   ____

Building Communication

A. Learn. *Look at the phrases below to learn how to use them.*

1. cut from the same cloth - The same or similar in characteristic or personality

   He and his sister are so alike. I guess they really are cut from the same cloth.

2. whereas - Compared to

   It seems like you don't care. Whereas I am taking this seriously.

3. depending on (____) - to be decided or changed by (____)

   I might stop and get a coffee during lunch, depending on the time.

B. Practice. *Complete the sentences with the phrases from above.*

1. ____________________ when we finish dinner, we might be able to catch a movie afterward.
2. Seoul doesn't get much snow in the winter, ____________________ Jeju Island gets quite a lot of snow.
3. I thought the new president would be different, but I was wrong. All these politicians are ____________________.

C. More Practice. *Make sentences using the phrases above.*

1. cut from the same cloth

   ____

2. whereas

   ____

3. depending on ~

   ____

Grammar: Modals of Probability

Modals of probability are used to talk about things that could happen or be true in the past, present, or future. They are added in front of the main verb. Which is used depends on how certain one is that the statement is true.

	Possible	*Impossible*
Very Certain	must *I smell fresh bread. There must be a bakery nearby.*	can't *This can't be his house. His house is brown, this one is blue.*
*Somewhat Certain**	might *I might go to the party if I finish my homework.*	must not *She must not be awake yet. She's not answering her phone.*
	may *I may go to the beach tomorrow.*	might not *It might not be a good day for a picnic. It's cloudy and chilly.*
Less Certain	could *I heard the party could be cancelled.*	may not *Mark may not join us for dinner.*

* *"Might" and "may" are of an equal level of certainty. However, "must not" is slightly more certain than "might not".*

A. Practice. ***Complete the sentences using a modal from above.***

1. She hasn't eaten since yesterday morning. She ____________ be so hungry!
2. I just talked to her on the phone and she said she was at work, so she ____________ be at home right now.
3. Tomorrow will be warmer than today. It ____________ snow tomorrow.

B. More Practice. ***Look at the picture below and write three (3) sentences containing modals of probability about the picture.***

1. ______________________________
____
2. ______________________________
____
3. ______________________________
____

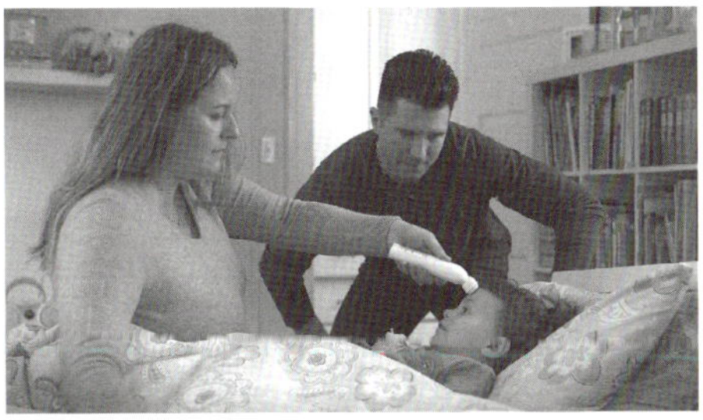

Speaking Skill: Alternative Perspectives

Alternative perspectives are different opinions or interpretations about a topic. You can use alternative perspectives to share, compare, contrast, or make your own argument stronger.

Step 1	Introduce the alternative perspective *Phrases*: Some argue that.../ Another interpretation is.../ The opposing side believes ...
Step 2	Compare or contrast the alternative perspective with your own *Phrases*: Similarly,.../ However,.../ On the other hand,...
Step 3 (optional)	Refute the opposing view and support your view *Use support to disprove the other side and support your side*

It's important to research alternative perspectives. If you're unsure, start with these questions:

What does the other side think? Why? What is their support?

What is the opposite of my view?

What are other possible interpretations of this issue?

A. Practice. ***Use the questions above to think of alternative perspectives for the following arguments.***

Argument Eight hours of sleep is essential for a healthy, productive life.

Alternative ______________________________

Perspective ______________________________

Argument Computer games are harmful to our mind and body.

Alternative ______________________________

Perspective ______________________________

B. More Practice. ***Choose 1 alternative perspective from above. Write and share 3-5 sentences using steps 1-3 and phrases.***

ex) Some argue that meat is unhealthy. However, most doctors recommend meat as part of a healthy diet. According to the World Health Organization, ...

____

____

Wrap-Up

A. Write & Talk. ***Practice asking and answering the questions below to have a conversation with a partner or group.***

1. What do you consider when you choose how you travel? Why?

____

____

2. Do you ever use low pollution methods of transportation? Why?

____

____

3. Have you ever travelled to another country and used their public transportation system? What was it like?

____

____

4. What are some advantages of transportation in your country? What are some of the drawbacks?

____

____

5. What do you think transportation will be like in the future?

____

____

B. Quiz. ***Take the quiz below to see how well you understood the unit.***

1. When buying their first home, the young couple __________ many different places, but their budget was small so they had to choose the most __________ place.

   a. encouraged, impact
   c. impact, drastically
   b. considered, affordable
   d. go about, impact

2. Transportation is changing due to technology as well as the impact it has on the __________.

   a. electricity
   c. cost

b. energy usage

d. environment

3. Our flight is in a few hours but there is a typhoon coming in. The airline hasn't made an announcement yet, but I think our flight __________ be cancelled. This is going to ruin all our plans!

a. can't

c. must

b. might

d. might not

4. It's hard to know which way of travelling is best. Driving your car all the time is more convenient but creates more pollution __________ public transportation is better for the environment but not always the best option.

a. depending on

c. whereas

b. according to

d. due to

5. You can make your argument or opinions stronger by __________.

a. including an alternative perspective

b. changing your argument often

c. ignoring those who do not agree with you

d. agreeing with other opinions

Notes. ***Use the space below to take notes on this unit.***

Unit 7

Take It Easy

In this Unit...

Vocabulary	Grammar
deal with, make-or-break, connotation, adolescent, bottle up, overwhelming, reach out, outweigh	Conjunctive Adverbs
Reading Topic	**Speaking Skill**
Stress and Mental Health	Reaching a Conclusion

Building Communication

have a tendency to, take a toll on, in the long run

Preview

A. Conversation. *Read the conversation below.*

Simone I have been so stressed lately...

Jorge You do deal with a lot of pressure from work and home. You've heard about a mental health vacation, haven't you?

Simone No, I haven't. What is that?

Jorge It's a break from social media or other things that stress you out.

Simone I relax at home on the weekends. For example, I watch a lot of Netflix.

Jorge Relaxing is good. However, it's not the same. Experts nowadays say that it's important to take breaks from high stress environments and actively try to relieve the stress you bottle up over time. For instance, not using social media for two days. Instead, read a book or go for walks or reach out to friends.

B. Warm-up. *Circle your top 5 sources of stress. What makes you feel stressed out?*

parents	school	part-time job
relationship	the future	money
the past	friends	transportation

C. Write & Discuss. *When you feel stress from these issues, what do you do to feel better? Write 2-3 sentences and share.*

___

___

___

Vocabulary Focus

A. Definition Matching. *Write the letter next to the correct word.*

______	1. deal with	A. about youth; young person
______	2. make-or-break	B. to be more important than
______	3. connotation	C. take action to solve a problem
______	4. adolescent	D. very strong emotional feeling
______	5. bottle up	E. keep negative feelings inside
______	6. overwhelming	F. contact someone
______	7. reach out	G. idea or feeling connected to a word
______	8. outweigh	H. main factor in success or failure

B. Fill in the Blanks. *Write the correct vocabulary word from above.*

1. I know you're really busy these days, so please ______________ if you need any help with anything!
2. Although buying a new house anytime is a bit risky, I think the benefits ______________ the risks right now.
3. ______________ social pressure is an important issue. We need to let young teenagers know that they don't have to follow others, and they can make their own healthy choices.
4. When we think about success, we often think long-term. However, it is really our daily habits that will ______________ our lifelong success.
5. When my friend told me the story of her boyfriend asking her to get married, the feeling was totally ______________ ! I'm happy for her.
6. I have so many things to do: homework, my part-time job, my friends... I don't want to ______________ all of this! I need a break.
7. When I learn a new word, I always consider two things: First, is this word common? Second, does it have any ______________ ?
8. It's better not to ______________ your emotions. If you're feeling upset, annoyed or angry, try to talk about it. You'll feel better.

Take It Easy

"Stress." What a terrible word, right? Even the word "Stress" can make us feel stressed out! Although most of us hate stress, it's a necessary part of life that we can't ignore. Stress can come from anywhere; school, work, friends, or family. Regardless of the source, what matters is how we deal with it. Recognizing positive stress, as well as developing realistic strategies in our lives to manage stress, can make-or-break our daily mental and physical health.

While the word stress has a negative connotation, research tells us that there are some positive aspects as well. Positive stress, known as "eustress" can help create new connections in the brain and, if viewed positively, can prepare us for a coming challenge. Despite these upsides, most people fall prey to negative stress at one time or another. Adolescent stress in Korea is largely related to family issues and academic performance. Pressure to do well in school is especially common. As we get older, job-related stress begins to replace the stress of education. New stresses, including money, housing, and health may pop up. Regardless of age, many of us *have a tendency to* bottle up stress or negative emotions. This, however, is the worst thing we can do. It *takes a toll on* our physical and mental health, creating a whole host of illnesses, ranging from headaches to heart problems.

While stress sometimes seems overwhelming, there are many ways to manage the stress that we can't avoid. A healthy work-life balance and avoiding burnout are important. Instead of bottling up your stress, find a way to release it. How? Try organizing your thoughts through journaling. Release your energy through sports or exercise. Reach out to friends, family, or talk to a therapist, who can help you to understand yourself and improve your mental health. Experiment with different activities, and find out what works for you. Taking care of yourself by practicing healthy stress habits will increase your mental strength, and you'll be healthier and more resilient *in the long run*.

Stress isn't entirely bad, but the negatives clearly outweigh the positives. Be aware of positive stress, but also be realistic about the negative stress in your life. Experiment and find the best way to manage it. However you choose to do it, don't let stress sneak up on you! Remember to unplug, decompress, and make time for yourself.

Comprehension Check

A. Summary. ***Fill each blank with information from the text.***

Stress is unavoidable; it's a fact of life. While there are many sources of stress, what is most important is how we ________________ it. Developing realistic ________________ to manage stress can help us to live a healthier life. While we mostly think of stress as negative, research tells us that there are also positive sides, such as preparing us for an upcoming ________________. However, stress from home, school, or work is mostly unhealthy. Many people will ________________ their stress, keeping their emotions inside and causing health issues. Instead, we can try to manage or release stress by organizing our thoughts through ________________, or releasing energy through exercise. Find what works best for you!

B. True/False. ***If the sentence is false, correct it to make it true.***

1. Positive stress is known as "eustress". (T/F)
2. Adolescent and adult stress come from the same sources. (T/F)
3. Stress causes many serious health problems. (T/F)
4. It's healthier to bottle up stress rather than release it. (T/F)
5. Everyone should find their own way to manage stress. (T/F)

C. Short Answer. ***Answer each question with information from the text.***

1. What are some negative health effects due to stress?

____

____

____

2. What are some ways to manage unavoidable stress mentioned in the reading?

____

____

____

Building Communication

A. Learn. *Look at the phrases below to learn how to use them.*

1. have a tendency to - usually do a certain behavior

   I really want to finish my work quickly, but actually, I have a tendency to do it at the last minute.

2. take a toll on - have a damaging effect over time

   I have been working in politics for over 20 years, and let me tell you: this job really takes a toll on you.

3. in the long run - over a long time, eventually

   Sure, alcohol is fun. But in the long run, it's not good for your health.

B. Practice. *Complete the sentences with the phrases from above.*

1. My sister ____________________ overreact, even when something small happens.
2. Getting only 4 or 5 hours of sleep each night really ______________ ______ your health. Make sure to prioritize sleep!
3. Although eating junk food isn't good for health, I think eating it occasionally isn't too bad ____________________.

C. More Practice. *Make sentences using the phrases above.*

1. have a tendency to ~

   ____

2. take a toll on ~

   ____

Grammar: Conjunctive Adverbs

Conjunctive adverbs are adverbs that go in the beginning of a sentence that show its relationship to the previous sentence.

Cause/Effect	*Time*	*Contrast*	*Sequence*
Accordingly	Before	However	First/Next
Consequently	Since	Instead	Finally
Therefore	Now	On the other hand	In addition
Then	Lately		Moreover
Summarize	***Emphasis***	***Comparison***	***Illustrate***
Briefly	Of course	Like/As	For example
In conclusion	Certainly	Likewise	For instance
In summary	Definitely	Similarly	
	Indeed	In contrast	

In writing, they can be used in two ways.

→ Jia kept talking in class. Therefore, she got in trouble.

→ Jia kept talking in class; therefore, she got in trouble.

A. Practice. ***Complete the sentences with a conjunctive adverb.***

1. She is a very smart woman; ________, she graduated top of her class in both high school and university.
2. John has very little money. ________, his brother is a millionaire.
3. We wanted to go to the beach; ________, it started to rain so we stayed home.
4. I love sweet food. ________, I always order desserts when I eat at a restaurant, even if I'm full.

B. More Practice. ***Write a summary of what you did last weekend, including at least three conjunctive adverbs.***

____

____

____

Speaking Skill: Reaching a Conclusion

A conclusion is your final opinion on a topic after researching it and considering alternative perspectives. Reaching a conclusion usually follows this process:

1. Begin with limited knowledge about the topic
2. Research the topic deeply
3. Consider alternative perspectives
4. Decide your conclusion

This process can be used whether you're deciding on a new government policy or simply where to eat dinner. Once you've reached your conclusion, you may need to consider how to write or present your conclusion. The following is a common conclusion structure:

Transition	Signal to audience that we are moving toward the end *Phrases*: In conclusion .../ To sum up ... / All in all ...
Summary	Restate your main idea and support *Phrases*: Today, we discussed .../ In this presentation ...
Call to Action (optional)	Give the listener a final action or thought
Thank You	Thank listener for their time and attention

A. Practice. ***Research or discuss one of the topics below. Then write an example conclusion and share.***

Best drama of all time
Best spicy food
Benefits of sunlight
Cola vs. Cider

ex) In conclusion, cider is better than cola. Today, we talked about how fresh and clean cider is, and how unhealthy cola is. So please drink cider! Thank you.

____

____

____

____

Wrap-Up

A. Write & Talk. ***Practice asking and answering the questions below to have a conversation with a partner or group.***

1. What are the main sources of stress in your life?

____

____

2. What are two healthy ways you could manage or release your stress?

____

____

3. How was your experience with stress in middle and high school? Did you feel extremely stressed out at a certain time?

____

____

4. What are two things you want to try to release or manage your stress?

____

____

5. When have you experienced eustress in your life?

____

____

B. Quiz. ***Take the quiz below to see how well you understood the unit.***

1. It's important to __________ stress as it comes instead of _____it ____. Otherwise, it will start to affect your health.
   a. reach out, dealing ... with
   b. deal with, bottling ... up
   c. bottle up, reaching ... out
   d. make-or-break, outweighing
2. Stress can have a negative impact on your life if you do not manage it well, but not all stress is bad. Stress that helps you prepare for oncoming challenges is called __________.
   a. a connotation
   b. nonstress
   c. stressful
   d. eustress

3. The young man spent his money on whatever he wanted; __________, he was unable to save enough and pay off his debts.

a. consequently
b. similarly
c. for example
d. instead

4. Sometimes, some situations can be very difficult, but if you stick with them, they can be very helpful __________.

a. in the long run
b. falling prey to
c. taking a toll on you
d. having a tendency

5. Which of the following is not one of the steps before you reach a conclusion?

a. disagree with others
b. research the topic
c. have limited knowledge of topic
d. consider alternative perspectives

Notes. ***Use the space below to take notes on this unit.***

Unit 8

To-may-to, To-mah-to

In this Unit...

Vocabulary	Grammar
inevitably, cultivate, confront, lose one's temper, irreconcilable, merit, narrow-minded, bias	Present/Past Perfect
Reading Topic	**Speaking Skill**
Importance of Differing Opinions	Nonverbal Communication

Building Communication
in the course of, take (it) into consideration, put yourself in one's shoes

Preview

A. Conversation. *Read the conversation below.*

Cecilia It's pretty hard to have conversations with people nowadays.

Joel Definitely. It seems like people are more narrow-minded than they used to be. I've had a hard time sharing my opinion with my family.

Cecilia I've had the same issue. I wish people listened to each other more.

Joel Me, too. I think it's because people are afraid to confront others or be wrong. But having discussions with others is how we learn and cultivate ourselves, right?

Cecilia You're absolutely right. I think we need to learn how to change our minds about a topic without feeling mad or like we are wrong.

Joel We would all be better if we could do that.

B. Warm-up. *Write 4 contentious topics that many people disagree on. How do you react when you disagree with someone? Do you share your opinion freely? Or do you hide your opinion to keep the atmosphere smooth?*

1. ______________________ 3. ______________________

2. ______________________ 4. ______________________

C. Write & Discuss. *Write 2-3 sentences about the last time you disagreed with someone. What was the issue? How did you react?*

____

____

____

Vocabulary Focus

A. Definition Matching. *Write the letter next to the correct word.*

______	1. inevitably	A. grow
______	2. cultivate	B. face or meet a difficult situation
______	3. confront	C. believing or supporting one side unfairly
______	4. lose one's temper	D. unavoidable, certain to happen
______	5. irreconcilable	E. a good, useful, or valuable point
______	6. merit	F. become angry, lose control
______	7. narrow-minded	G. impossible to agree or compromise
______	8. bias	H. not accepting different opinions or ideas

B. Fill in the Blanks. *Write the correct vocabulary word from above.*

1. At first, my friend and I liked different baseball teams. I thought our differences were ______________, but now we just enjoy watching the game.
2. My dad still drinks the same beer from the old days. He refuses to try anything else. He's so ______________!
3. Even though we disagree, I think your idea has ______________. Maybe we can use it in the future.
4. In the same way that we can grow flowers or weeds in a garden, we can ______________our mind to be a peaceful place or a stressful place.
5. When I saw my friend steal ice cream from the convenience store, I had to ______________ him. He apologized and put it back.
6. Sometimes, my dog escapes our house and runs away. But he ______________ returns when he gets tired and hungry.
7. The application process is completely free of ______________. We select our employees on merit alone.
8. When I was younger, I used to ______________ a lot, even about small things, especially computer games. Now, I control my emotions well.

To-may-to, To-mah-to

In the course of our daily lives, we inevitably run into different ideas, opinions, and perspectives. We cannot learn language without also learning about the culture of the people who speak it, and as we do, we often discover beliefs that may be different than our own. They may be as small as differences in fashion or music, or as vast as different religious worldviews. We can develop a few key strategies to deal with these situations. Cultivating self-awareness, seeking to understand ourselves and others, and engaging in open and honest communication will result in deeper understanding.

We're all born into a society and culture that is deeply influenced by history, religion, politics, and war. That history might encourage us to look down on a certain ethnicity, stereotype a certain group of people, or hate a certain country. When confronted with these differences, it's easy to lose our temper. Why? Because, at first, some differences seem irreconcilable. However, most differences in life can be overcome by carefully considering our own views, the views of others, and finding a way to move forward together. Making an effort to understand the gaps in our own knowledge, while also seeking the potential merits in others' ideas, can increase our understanding of people, culture, and the nature of belief. Try to *take* their opinion *into consideration*.

We also find those with whom we disagree in our own cultures as well. You might meet someone with different political beliefs. Stop and think: is their opinion truly worse? Am I being narrow-minded? In some cases, you'll decide your way is better—and you might be right! The essential lesson is to realize that we all have certain biases, whether from our cultures or personal experiences. Awareness of these biases—how they're formed and how they determine our worldviewis an important part of understanding ourselves.

When we run into different ideas and opinions, our calm may be shaken and our tempers lost. Before you get upset and defensive, *put yourself in their shoes*. Take others' opinions into consideration, and try to understand where they're coming from.

Comprehension Check

A. Summary. ***Fill each blank with information from the text.***

In life, we're going to run into people with different opinions, ideas, and beliefs. This is especially true when studying a foreign ________________ . Language and culture are closely connected, giving us different opinions on politics, fashion, or religious ________________. This means that we will sometimes lose our temper when discussing sensitive issues. However, if we consider our own views and the views of others, we can find a way to ________________ together. Making this effort can increase our ________________ of people and beliefs. Of course, we can disagree with our own friends and family as well. But the same answer applies: ________________ : is their opinion truly worse? Am I missing something? Am I biased? Honest communication and keeping an open mind will bring us awareness and better understanding.

B. True/False. ***If the sentence is false, correct it to make it true.***

1. Language can be learned without culture. (T/F)
2. All societies and cultures have been influenced by history. (T/F)
3. All differences are irreconcilable. (T/F)
4. Considering the other person's side can help understanding. (T/F)
5. It's better to keep a closed mind rather than an open mind. (T/F)

C. Short Answer. ***Answer each question with information from the text.***

1. What are societies and cultures influenced by? Which do you think is the strongest influence?

____

____

2. Write one strong opinion you have about pop culture.

____

____

Building Communication

A. Learn. *Look at the phrases below to learn how to use them.*

1. in the course of - during, throughout

   There have been so many disasters in the course of human history.

2. take (it) into consideration - think about carefully

   A: *If you're not happy, you should change your major.*

   B: *Yeah, maybe. I'll take it into consideration.*

3. put yourself in one's shoes - imagine her opinion or problem

   A: *I really don't understand how she can think that way.*

   B: *Well, put yourself in her shoes. She might have some trauma.*

B. Practice. *Complete the sentences with the phrases from above.*

1. I know it's inconvenient, but we need to ______ everyone's schedule ____________________. The time should be possible for everyone.
2. When my opinions are the opposite of my friend's, I try to ____________________ and understand his perspective.
3. We will have both struggles and victories ________________________ our lives.

C. More Practice. *Make sentences using the phrases above.*

1. in the course of ~

   ____

2. take ~ into consideration

   ____

3. put yourself in one's shoes

   ____

Grammar: Present/Past Perfect

There are three verb tenses used to talk about past events in English: *simple past, present perfect, and past perfect.*

Simple Past	Present Perfect	Past Perfect
Actions that started and completed at a known time in the past	*Actions that happened in the past and continues to present or happened at an unknown time in the past*	*Actions that happened at some unknown time in the past prior to another action*
→ We lived there for three years. (Don't live there anymore)	→ We have lived there for three years. (Still live there).	→ We had lived there for three years. (*Before moving or some other action*)

A. Practice. ***Choose the correct form of the verb in parentheses to complete the sentences.***

1. By the time I got to the room, the meeting ________ (*start, already*) without me. The boss ________ (*be*) mad at me.
2. When Suzy ________ (*walk*) into the room, I ________ (*recognize, not*) her because she ________ (*lose*) a lot of weight and ________ (*cut*) her hair.
3. Julian ________ (*visit*) so many beautiful places since he ________ (*come*) to Korea. Before moving here, he ________ (*see, never*) such beautiful temples and palaces.

B. More Practice. ***Create a short story for how this couple fell in love using all three past tense grammars.***

____

____

____

____

Speaking Skill: Nonverbal Communication

Communication is not always verbal. Nonverbal communication, sometimes known as body language, includes posture, gestures and facial expressions. In fact, more than half of our communication is nonverbal! Here are some common types of positive and negative body language.

	Positive	Negative
Posture	Shoulder back, head high	Slouching, eyes downward
Gestures	Open palms, active hands	Wringing hands, touching hair
Facial Expressions	Eye contact, warm smile, relaxed facial muscles	Avoiding eye contact, frown, empty expression

Tip: When we feel nervous, we often show certain nonverbal communication unconsciously, i.e., pulling hair behind the ear, touching glasses, moving hands or legs unnaturally. Ask your classmates to help you identify these traits, sometimes known as nervous tics.

A. Practice. *Find a short video online of a presentation (in English or Korean). With your team, identify the body language and tics of the speaker. Is their body language good or bad?*

B. More Practice. *Write a short role-play about any topic with your team. Add actions after each line of dialogue that describes body language. Ex. He looked away. She rolled her eyes. He straightened his glasses.*

Wrap-Up

A. Write & Talk. ***Practice asking and answering the questions below to have a conversation with a partner or group.***

1. What are 2 strongly held beliefs or opinions you have about life?

   ____

   ____

2. Imagine you met someone who disagreed with one of your opinions from the first question. What would you say?

   ____

   ____

3. Have you ever lost your temper with a friend? About what?

   ____

   ____

4. How do you feel when you interact with people from other cultures?

   ____

   ____

5. Write about a time when you realized your opinion was wrong and you changed your mind. How did it feel? Was it easy or difficult?

   ____

   ____

B. Quiz. ***Take the quiz below to see how well you understood the unit.***

1. People who have a ________ towards a certain way of thinking tend to be very ________ and not open to considering others' opinions.

   a. merit, irreconcilable　　c. confront, narrow-minded

   b. impulse, inevitably　　d. bias, narrow-minded

2. When interacting with other people, you will always meet others who ________ with you. However, instead of ignoring their opinion, it's important to consider it and try to learn from it.

   a. agree　　c. argue

b. disagree

d. consider

3. When making a big life decision, Maria's father told her to __________ what the consequences will be beforehand.

a. in the course of

c. take into consideration

b. run contrary to

d. put yourself in one's shoes

4. Kelly was sick but didn't have time to go to the doctor and get a prescription, so she went to the pharmacy and got some __________ medicine to help with her fever.

a. PIN

c. OTC

b. widget

d. RN

5. Which of the following is not a nonverbal communication method?

a. voice

c. gestures

b. posture

d. facial expressions

Notes. ***Use the space below to take notes on this unit.***

Unit 9

Preparing for Tomorrow

In this Unit...

Vocabulary	Grammar
helpless, ins-and-outs, budget, lucrative, keep track of, exponential, pitfall, be wary of	Present Perfect Continuous
Reading Topic	**Speaking Skill**
Financial Security	Responding to News from Others

Building Communication

at all costs, too good to be true, don't beat oneself up

Preview

A. Conversation. *Read the conversation below.*

Brian Hey, Jen. How is your budget going?

Jen It's so tough. Fall season is here, but I can't buy any new clothes.

Brian Yeah, I know how you feel. I've been trying to keep track of my money as well. It's not easy.

Jen Right!? I have to be wary of buying anything expensive. I even decided to stop buying my daily coffee in order to save more.

Brian No way! That's terrible. But you might be right. I probably spend a lot of money on small things like coffee.

Jen Yeah. I've been carefully analyzing my spending habits and making some tough choices. Coffee was really hard to give up...

Brian You're stronger than me! I couldn't do it. I'm totally helpless without caffeine!

B. Warm-up. *Think about your spending then write the four things you buy most often.*

How do you spend your money? Do you have expensive taste?
Do you buy small, cheap things often?

1. ______________________ 3. ______________________
2. ______________________ 4. ______________________

C. Write & Discuss. *Write about the most expensive thing you ever bought. Was it worth it? How did you feel before and after buying it?*

____

____

____

Vocabulary Focus

A. Definition Matching. *Write the letter next to the correct word.*

_______ 1. helpless	A. continue to be informed about
_______ 2. ins-and-outs	B. a hidden danger
_______ 3. budget	C. important details and facts
_______ 4. keep track of	D. feel or show caution
_______ 5. exponential	E. increasing or growing quickly
_______ 6. pitfall	F. unable to act, powerless
_______ 7. be wary of	G. producing a lot of money
_______ 8. lucrative	H. a plan to save or spend money

B. Fill in the Blanks. *Write the correct vocabulary word from above.*

1. I really want to learn how to play badminton, but I don't know how. Can you teach me the ________________ ?
2. Saving all of your money might seem like a good idea, but it could be a ________________. You should also think about investing some.
3. There are so many new games these days! It's impossible to __________ _______ them all.
4. When making big life decisions, you need to ________________ the consequences.
5. You need to learn about money when you're young. If you don't, you'll be completely ________________ in your old age.
6. The local government made a special ________________ for a new park.
7. The phone application business has had ________________ growth over the past 10 years.
8. Opening a small cafe might seem like fun, but usually it's not a very ________________ business.

Preparing for Tomorrow

Money: without it, we're helpless. In the modern world, money is required for nearly everything. So, how can we make it? How should we spend it? Financial education in schools is either uncommon or absent. Our parents might teach us about money, or they might not. We know that we need a job, but that's only the first step! Learning the ins-and-outs of earning, saving, and investing money can determine whether you'll spend your future in a cardboard box or in luxury. So let's get down to business.

Maybe you have a part-time job. You want to spend your hard-earned money, right? On what? A new phone? Cosmetics? Stock in a company? Bitcoin? A good place to start is by making a budget. How? First, you can analyze your spending habits. How much do you spend on coffee per month? On food, alcohol, and transport? Make a list and keep track of your spending habits for a month. When you know where your money is going, you can take the next step: make some financial goals. How much do you want to save per month? What spending habits can you cut? What can't you live without?

Once you get control of your budget and goals, you can begin to plan your financial future. Think long-term, not short-term. Compound interest, which is the exponential growth of reinvested interest over time, is a powerful tool. For example, let's imagine you buy a stock of Samsung. If you reinvest your earned interest to the initial principle, even your interest will earn interest! In other words, your money will continue to grow even if you do nothing. You'll also want to learn which pitfalls to avoid along the way. For example, you'll probably want to avoid credit card debt *at all costs*. Be wary of scams and issues like identity theft. While an investment opportunity might seem lucrative, be extra cautious if it seems *too good to be true*.

This advice doesn't mean that you can't enjoy your life; it just means: be aware and make small, good choices consistently. Ask yourself: Do I really need this? *Don't beat yourself up* over buying a coffee, but keep your choices in mind. Make smart choices now, and you'll be rich in your golden years!

Comprehension Check

A. Summary. ***Fill each blank with information from the text.***

Like it or not, money is an essential part of life. ______________ education in schools is uncommon or absent, so we need to learn this important topic from family or for ourselves. The first step is to analyze your ______________ habits. This will show you where your money is going. When you write it down, you can see clearly, and you might want to make some changes. When making your budget, it's better to think ______________ rather than short-term. Learning about investing and ______________ interest will also help your future planning. Try to avoid ______________ and be wary of scams. Make small, smart choices now, and you'll thank yourself later!

B. True/False. ***If the sentence is false, correct it to make it true.***

1. Financial education is common in schools. (T/F)
2. The first step is to make a budget. (T/F)
3. Compound interest isn't a helpful tool. (T/F)
4. It's better to avoid pitfalls along the way. (T/F)
5. Making 1 or 2 good choices is enough. (T/F)

C. Short Answer. ***Answer each question with information from the text.***

1. What are the three main steps for financial planning?

____

____

2. What is compound interest?

____

____

Building Communication

A. Learn. ***Look at the phrases below to learn how to use them.***

1. at all costs - regardless of difficulty or cost, no matter what

   A: *The flight time you want is very expensive. Is it okay?*

   B: *I don't care! I need to get to Jeju at all costs!*

2. too good to be true - so good it's hard to believe, suspicious

   A new BMW for 5000 dollars? Sounds too good to be true.

3. don't beat oneself up - don't criticize yourself too much

   A: *I totally failed the exam...*

   B: *Hey, don't beat yourself up. It was really tough.*

B. Practice. ***Read the sentence/conversation below and complete the sentences with the phrases from above.***

1. It's okay to make mistakes. ________________________. Trying and failing is the only way to improve.
2. I recommend avoiding sugar ________________________. It's small food, but it makes you gain weight quickly.
3. A diet that includes chocolate cake!? That sounds __________________ __________!

C. More Practice. ***Make sentences using the phrases above.***

1. at all costs

   ____

2. too good to be true

   ____

3. don't beat oneself up

   ____

Grammar: Present Perfect Continuous

The present perfect continuous (or progressive) verb tense is used to show an action that started in the past and is continuing at the present time. It usually follows the form: have/has + been + -ing. For example:

My sister has been working at the company for 6 months.

I haven't been feeling well recently.

This verb indicates that the action and time period is still ongoing. It is especially common when talking about "recently", "these days" or "nowadays" Occasionally, it is used with a recently finished action that affects the present:

She's tired because she's been studying all night.

Oh, the sidewalk is wet. Has it been raining?

This verb tense can be used in similar situations as present perfect, but they are not the same. Present perfect is more often used with finished actions and stative verbs, while present perfect continuous is used for ongoing actions. For some verbs (study, live, work) both verb tenses can be used.

A. Practice. *Complete the sentences with present perfect continuous.*

1. ________________ (*my best friend/live*) in Canada for 5 years.
2. The exam is tomorrow. ________________ (*I/study*) for a month. I really hope I pass!
3. ________________ (*he/work*) late recently?
4. Your eyes are red. ________________ (*you/cry*)?
5. I really think ________________ (*I/drink*) too much coffee recently. I need to cut back.

B. More Practice. *Write a full sentence using present perfect continuous with the pair of subjects and verbs below.*

1. (My parents/work)

____

2. (I/watch)

____

3. (He/play)

____

Speaking Skill: Responding to News from Others

Short, verbal responses to the news and stories of others are an important part of natural conversations. Using neutral phrases such as *"OK"*, *"Uh-huh"* and *"Right"* will let others know you're following their words. You can then respond to their news, stories or information in the following ways:

Good	Bad	Surprising
That's great! / amazing!/wonderful!	Oh no!	Really?
How cool!	Oh, that's awful./ That's terrible.	No way!
I'm happy to hear that.	What a shame.	Are you serious?
Aw, I'm so glad.	I'm so sorry.	You're joking!

Using the above phrases during a conversation will let the speaker know that you're listening, understanding and sympathizing with their story. This will keep the conversation moving naturally.

A. Practice. ***Read the conversation and write an appropriate phrase.***

Sara Erin, I have bad news. I broke up with my boyfriend last night.

Erin ________________ What happened?

Sara I saw him at a cafe with another girl. It was Minhee.

Erin ________________ How could he do that? And with Minhee

Sara I don't know. I thought everything was fine.

Erin Well, I'm sorry to hear that, but I also have some news.

Sara ________________ Tell me something positive!

Erin I passed my license exam! So I can get a job now.

Sara ________________

B. More Practice. ***Write a short conversation about 2 friends sharing stories from last weekend. Use the phrases from above.***

____

____

____

Wrap-Up

A. Write & Talk. ***Practice asking and answering the questions below to have a conversation with a partner or group.***

1. How much money do you usually spend each month? On what?

____

____

2. What's the last expensive thing bought? Are you still happy with it?

____

____

3. What activities, actions, or habits do you try to avoid at all costs?

____

____

4. What do you want to get a hold on in your life?

____

____

5. If you wanted to save as much money as possible, how would you make a budget to achieve that goal?

____

____

B. Quiz. ***Take the quiz below to see how well you understood the unit.***

1. __________ how much you spend is necessary if you don't want to go over your __________.

   a. Being wary of, budget
   b. Budgeting, pitfall
   c. Lucrative, ins-and-outs
   d. Keeping track of, budget

2. After you start making money, it's important to make __________ for yourself and then work towards them by saving and investing your money smartly.

   a. financial goals
   b. pitfalls
   c. spending habits
   d. credit card debt

3. My grandmother fell for another telephone scam! I keep telling her if it seems __________, then it must be!

a. at all costs
b. to get a hold on
c. too good to be true
d. don't beat yourself up

4. We __________ here since the early 2000s and I don't see us moving anytime soon.

a. lived
b. have lived
c. live
d. had lived

5. __________ is a way to respond to positive news from others.

a. You're joking.
b. Oh no!
c. How cool!
d. What a shame.

Notes. ***Use the space below to take notes on this unit.***

Unit 10

A Little R & R

In this Unit...

Vocabulary	Grammar
fulfilling, pastime, wages, slave away, recreational, binge (watch), be into, downtime	Context Clues
Reading Topic	**Speaking Skill**
Leisure Trends	Circumventing

Building Communication
hard to come by, in the spotlight, take ___ by storm

Preview

A. Conversation. *Read the conversation below.*

Sunhwa Ah, it's Friday! I'm happy to finally have some downtime. I've been so busy lately. What are you up to this weekend, Alex?

Alex Same here. I'm really into this new game, so I can't wait to spend all day Saturday playing!

Sunhwa Nice! I'm gonna spend all day Saturday binge watching the entire new season of my drama on Netflix. But I think I'll go out and get some exercise on Sunday.

Alex What are you gonna do? Do you have any special hobbies?

Sunhwa It's not mine, exactly, but my dad's pastime is hiking. So I think I'll go hiking with him for a few hours.

Alex Sounds fun. I should get some exercise, too+but+

Sunhwa Don't waste your whole weekend! Do something fulfilling!

B. Warm-up. *Circle the top 3 activities you'd like to try and compare with others.*

When was the last time you tried a new hobby?

Baking	Surfing	Hiking
Birdwatching	Meditation	Painting
Writing	Camping	Yoga

C. Write & Discuss. *Share three hobbies you would never want to try.*

1. ______________________________
2. ______________________________
3. ______________________________

Vocabulary Focus

A. Definition Matching. *Write the letter next to the correct word.*

_______	1. fulfilling	A. do a lot quickly without stopping
_______	2. pastime	B. work very hard continuously
_______	3. wages	C. making one feel happy and satisfied
_______	4. slave away	D. payment to a worker
_______	5. recreational	E. time to relax and rest
_______	6. binge (watch)	F. enjoy or like something a lot
_______	7. be into _____	G. hobby
_______	8. downtime	H. related to activities for fun or enjoyment

B. Fill in the Blanks. *Write the correct vocabulary word from above.*

1. Did you see that new TV show? It's so good! I ________________ the entire first season in one day!
2. Despite increasing prices, workers' ________________ have remained the same for the last two years.
3. My sister works as a nurse. She said the schedule is tough, but the job of helping people is very ________________ .
4. Birdwatching has been my dad's ________________ for many years. He brings his binoculars everywhere we go!
5. My husband and I just had our second baby, so we're really busy. I don't have much ________________ these days.
6. During the holidays, most people are ________________ in the kitchen preparing food for family members who come to visit.
7. I enjoy playing all kinds of sports. I'm not that good at physical activity, so it's just ________________ for me.
8. My younger brother ________________ computer games. He won't go outside, so many parents are a little worried.

A Little R & R

Wouldn't it be nice to have a day off whenever you wanted? Sounds great, doesn't it? For most people, free time is a little *hard to come by*. So when we have it, we want to enjoy it to the fullest. But how we enjoy our free time depends on us. Would you rather take a bike ride or spend the afternoon in a cafe? Hike a mountain or lay in bed all day? While 'leisure' can be as simple as laying in bed, you can also make your free time as fulfilling as possible by trying out a bunch of fun activities that are growing in popularity.

The word "leisure" comes from the Old French word *leisir* and Latin *licere*, and means free or idle time. How people spend their leisure time has changed over the centuries. Originally a pastime for the upper classes and nobility, leisure as a concept emerged in Europe when normal workers' wages increased and their working hours decreased. Suddenly, the poor who had slaved away seven days a week had spending money and spare time. What to do? In France, drinking, gambling, and singing clubs emerged; in Britain, sports like golf and cricket, theaters, and travel to seaside resorts began. As industrialization and development continued throughout the 20th century, a similar pattern emerged across the globe.

Things aren't so different today, are they? People have always enjoyed getting some R&R by spending time in nature. We still enjoy relaxing on the beach, or hiking the local mountain. But as Korea has taken its place among the world's developed nations and economies, new leisure activities have come *into the spotlight*. Travel to the seaside towns has been popular for a while, but now surfing is *taking* Korea *by storm*. Surf shops and schools have popped up in Yangyang and Jeju. Other recreational activities like birdwatching or paddle boarding are less popular, but have a devoted following. If those things sound too active, you might be the type to binge watch the new season of your favorite show, or hit the PC room to play a game that you are super into. Or maybe you simply prefer window shopping at the department store and a good cup of coffee.

We all need some downtime now and then. And it's perfectly okay to be a couch potato sometimes. But if you feel up to it, why not try something new? There's a lot out there waiting to be discovered! Get out there and give it a shot!

Comprehension Check

A. Summary. ***Fill each blank with information from the text.***

Although most people are busy students or have full-time jobs, we all have a bit of free time to enjoy. There are many new leisure activities growing in ________________ these days. The word "leisure" comes from the Old French word leisir which means free or ________________ time. Workers suddenly had free time, and leisure activities that were originally for the upper classes called ________________ popped up to occupy their time. Things are still similar today. As Korea has become more prosperous, new pastimes have appeared. For example, ________________ is taking Korea by storm. Of course, you can always just relax with a TV show or a game. Whatever you choose, enjoy your time!

B. True/False. ***If the sentence is false, correct it to make it true.***

1. "Leisure" comes from an old German word. (T/F)
2. Leisure as a concept emerged in Europe. (T/F)
3. In France, sports like golf and cricket became popular. (T/F)
4. Surfing has become more popular in Korea. (T/F)
5. It's better to have an active hobby. (T/F)

C. Short Answer. ***Answer each question with information from the text.***

1. Where does the word "leisure" come from?

____

____

2. Which activities in the reading are for less active people?

____

____

Building Communication

A. Learn. ***Look at the phrases below to learn how to use them.***

1. hard to come by - difficult to find

   I've been looking for the special edition of this phone but it's really hard to come by.

2. in the spotlight - to get a lot of attention

   The actor has been in the spotlight recently because his new movie was released last week.

3. take ____ by storm - quickly become popular or successful

   A: *K-Pop is becoming popular all over the place...*

   B: *Yeah. It's really taking the world by storm!*

B. Practice. ***Complete the sentences with the phrases from above.***

1. It seems like Elon Musk is always ____________________ these days.
2. I want to buy the car, but the color that I want, mint green, is really ______________________.
3. Every year, it seems that some new winter fashion, usually a jacket, _______ Korea ______________.

C. More Practice. ***Make sentences using the phrases above.***

1. hard to come by

   ____

2. in the spotlight

   ____

3. take ~ by storm

   ____

Grammar: Context Clues

Context Clues are clues in grammar or a situation that help someone figure out the meaning of an unknown word. There are two types.

Linguistic		Situational	
Synonym/ Antonym	words around the unknown word that have similar/ opposite meanings	***Cause/ Effect***	relationship between unknown words and other parts of the sentence
Examples	examples of the unknown word	***Topic***	knowledge about a topic
Root Words	a smaller word part that is used to make other larger words	***Culture***	knowledge about a culture or culture's way of speaking
Parts of Speech	grammatical parts of speech (i.e. prefix, suffix, etc.)	***Comparis ons***	comparison to similar or dissimilar things

Context clues can be used alone or together to be more effective.

A. Practice. ***Use context clues to guess the meaning of the bold words. Then, compare them to the actual definition.***

Conversation 1	*Conversation 2*
A: I was wondering, did you get that card you wanted?	A: Fatima, did you hear the company's new COVID policy?
B: I did but it wasn't easy. I had to **negotiate** with the guy to convince him to sell it to me.	B: No, what is it?
A: He didn't want to sell it?	A: To keep everyone safe, we are going to **telecommute** from home starting next week.
B: Not at first, but after I offered him a higher price, he sold it to me.	B: Oh, thanks. I'll really save time in the mornings.

	Conversation 1	*Conversation 2*
Context clue(s)		
Meaning (guess)		
Meaning (actual)		

Speaking Skill: Circumventing

To circumvent means to "go around". Circumventing is a useful skill when you want to "go around" a word you don't know, information you can't remember, or a sensitive topic. Here are 3 strategies you can use:

Descriptive Language	Synonyms/Antonyms	Comparisons
Talk about details, especially appearance: color, shape, size, feeling taste (5 senses) Use adjectives!	Synonym: A different word with the same (or similar) meaning Antonym: A different word with the opposite meaning	Think of similar or opposite words. Use "be+like" and "but"to show contrast. I.e. "It's like a tree, but smaller."

A. Practice. ***Fill-in the following conversations using any type of circumventing. Consider which type is best for each case.***

Minhee I'm really craving man-du. You know man-du? It's Korean food.

Ashley Um, I'm not sure. What is man-du?

Minhee ____.

Lisa Have you seen the new James Bond movie?

Justin No, not yet. How was it?

Lisa It was... I forgot the word. It's similar to ____________________ ______________________________________(amazing).

B. Extra Practice. ***Pick up an object nearby: your phone, book, pencil, etc.. Close your eyes. How could you describe this object to a friend without using that word (phone, book, etc.)? Try to use the 3 ways of circumventing to describe the object to a friend.***

____

____

Wrap-Up

A. Write & Talk. ***Practice asking and answering the questions below to have a conversation with a partner or group.***

1. How much free time do you have each week?

____

____

2. What are your top 2 hobbies that you spend the most time on?

____

____

3. What new hobbies have you heard about recently?

____

____

4. Are you active in your free time or do you prefer to just relax?

____

____

5. What do you like to do when you're a couch potato?

____

____

B. Quiz. ***Take the quiz below to see how well you understood the unit.***

1. Most people __________ at their jobs day to day without getting much __________ to enjoy themselves.

   a. are into, pastime
   c. slave away, downtime
   b. fulfilling, recreational
   d. binge watch, wages

2. How people spend their leisure time is always changing, but one thing that has always stayed the same is that people like to spend time in __________.

   a. their homes
   c. at work
   b. nature
   d. the mountains

3. Which of the following is not a type of context clue?

a. synonyms/antonyms
b. comparisons
c. cause/effect
d. relationship

4. Starting to collect something new is always fun, unless you are into collecting older things, then a lot of the more interesting items are __________.

a. a bunch of
b. hard to come by
c. into the spotlight
d. taking people by storm

5. Which of the following is not a way to circumvent using a word you don't know?

a. descriptive language
b. ignoring
c. comparisons
d. synonyms/antonyms

Notes. ***Use the space below to take notes on this unit.***

Unit 11

What Do You Do Again?

In this Unit...

Vocabulary	Grammar
pop up, strategist, interaction, represent, ethical, emerging, automation, keep up	Embedded Questions
Reading Topic	**Speaking Skill**
Careers	Active Listening

Building Communication

sing a different tune, have/has resulted in, keep up (get) with the times

Preview

A. Conversation. *Read the conversation below.*

Erin	Mark, do you know whether or not that new cafe is open yet?
Mark	I think it opened last week. There are so many new stores emerging around here these days, it's hard to keep up.
Erin	Yeah, that's true. But I think you should try the cafe. They have great coffee and their cake is good, too.
Mark	I see. So you're saying that their stuff is good quality?
Erin	Haha. Well, actually, I'm their social media strategist. I manage their Instagram page and website.
Mark	Oh, wow. That sounds like a cool job. Do you have to interact with a lot of people online?
Erin	I just take pictures, post content and answer some comments!

B. Warm-up. *Write 4 unique jobs of people you know. If you're not sure, search online.*

Do you know anyone with a really unique job?

What are some unique jobs that you might be happy doing?

1. ______________________ 3. ______________________
2. ______________________ 4. ______________________

C. Write & Discuss. *Write 2-3 sentences about one of the jobs above that you would like. Why does it seem fun? Would you really do it?*

____

____

____

Vocabulary Focus

A. Definition Matching. *Write the letter next to the correct word.*

_______ 1. pop up	A. operation by machine without human labor
_______ 2. strategist	B. be morally acceptable
_______ 3. interaction	C. be a symbol or image of something
_______ 4. represent	D. to suddenly occur or appear
_______ 5. ethical	E. maintain; continue without interruption
_______ 6. emerging	F. a person who plans the best course of action
_______ 7. automation	G. actions done amongst people or groups
_______ 8. keep up	H. becoming known or coming into existence

B. Fill in the Blanks. *Write the correct vocabulary word from above.*

1. The company hired a ________________ to help them decide the best way to promote their new brand.
2. The athletes were proud to ________________ their country at the Olympics.
3. The situation was still ________________ so there wasn't a lot of information available on the news about it.
4. Phillip was not able to ________________ with the quick pace of the class, so he asked the teacher for help.
5. The girl still felt shy around her classmates because they haven't had many ________________, so they still felt like strangers.
6. The researchers' methods for obtaining information were harmful to the subjects so they were considered to not be ________________.
7. People are always pleasantly surprised when they lose a sock and months later it ________________ in a random place.
8. Many people are worried they will lose their jobs to immigrants but a lot of companies don't hire as many people as before since technology has improve ___________.

What Do You Do Again?

If you asked a child twenty years ago what they wanted to be when they grew up, they probably would have told you a doctor or a fireman. Ask a kid nowadays what they would like to be and they'll probably be *singing a very different tune*. Although we still need doctors and firemen, countless new jobs have popped up that didn't exist in the past.

A lot of human interactions and businesses have moved online. As a result, there are many jobs that people have now that simply weren't possible before. So, what kind of job may some of today's kids have? Social media is a huge part of people's daily lives, so a lot of new jobs can be found there. For example, a social media strategist is a person who plans how companies should represent themselves on the Internet to best develop their brands. A similar job is data analyst. Businesses have to consider a lot of data when they make decisions. It can be difficult to understand all of the different information, so data analysts take the information, look for patterns, and present it to companies in a way they can use. If you have good computer skills, then maybe you'd be a good ethical hacker. Ethical hackers are people who break into a company's online security system to look for weaknesses.

Besides the Internet, other changes in society *have resulted in* many different kinds of work like these emerging and others disappearing. Some reports have shown that due to automation, over forty percent of businesses plan to replace people with machines that can do the same job. This means that fewer jobs will exist in the future. The job market is also responding to changes in what society thinks is important. Many countries around the world believe that we need to develop alternative sources of energy, such as solar and electric, and reduce our impact on the environment. As a result, jobs in fossil fuel energy have begun to disappear while new jobs in solar and electric energy have appeared. With all these new types of jobs being created, workers will need new skills and training to be able to work in the future. Jobs will require more critical thinking and technological skills that require special training. Today's workers may need to develop these new skill sets to *keep up with the times*.

As these jobs and changes become a bigger part of our daily lives, you may hear tomorrow's children talk about wanting a job you've never even heard of!

Comprehension Check

A. Summary. ***Fill each blank with information from the text.***

Kids today want to have very different ________________ compared to kids of the past. This is largely due to the advancement of the ________________. An example of a job that didn't exist before is a social media ________________ or a data ________________. Another one of these new jobs is a ________________ hacker, or person who looks for weaknesses in a company's ________________ system. There have also been changes to jobs thanks to other factors. One factor is ________________. This has led to a reduction of jobs for humans. Changing from fossil fuels to ________________ sources of energy has created new jobs. These changes in jobs will require workers to have more ________________ and special ________________.

B. True/False. ***If the sentence is false, correct it to make it true.***

1. Popular jobs among young people have not changed recently. (T/F)
2. Many new jobs are a result of the Internet. (T/F)
3. Nowadays, there are fewer jobs for people because machines are able to do the same jobs. (T/F)
4. The job market determines what society believes is important. (T/F)
5. Jobs in the future will require simpler, easier to develop skills. (T/F)

C. Short Answer. ***Answer each question with information from the text.***

1. What are some jobs that exist today thanks to the Internet that did not exist 100 years ago?

   ____

   ____

2. What other changes in society have resulted in the creation of new jobs?

   ____

   ____

Building Communication

A. Learn. *Look at the phrases below to learn how to use them.*

1. sing a different tune - change one's opinion or attitude

   You may think living in the countryside is fun, but you'll be singing a different tune when you are bored in the middle of nowhere.

2. have/has resulted in - cause something to happen

   The changes that the company made have resulted in increased profits.

3. keep up (get) with the times - update old knowledge

   A: *Huh? You can pay for coffee with your phone?*

   B: *Are you serious? Get with the times*, man!

B. Practice. *Complete the sentences with the phrases from above.*

1. You may think money isn't that important when you're young, but you'll be ____________________ when you're older!
2. I was talking to my dad and he asked me what YouTube is! I had to tell him to ____________________!
3. The decrease in demand for books ____________________ many bookstores moving to an online only model.

C. More Practice. *Make sentences using the phrases above.*

1. sing a different tune

   ____

2. have (has) resulted in

   ____

3. keep up with the times

   ____

Grammar: Embedded Questions

Embedded questions are questions that can be found inside another question or statement (sentence).

They are made up of two parts: an *introductory phrase* and a *main question*. How you join the *main question* to the *introductory phrase* depends on the type of question:

Yes/No	Wh- Question
Will he be coming tomorrow?	What is the answer to the question?
if/whether (or not) + subject + verb	Wh-word + subject + verb
Do you know whether or not he will be coming tomorrow?	*I don't know what the answer to the question is.*

A. Practice. ***Combine the following parts to make embedded questions/ sentences.***

1. What time does the doctor's office open? (Can you tell me?)

   ____

2. How long does it take to get to the beach from here? (Do you remember?)

   ____

3. What does "aye-aye" mean? (I'm not sure...)

   ____

B. More Practice. ***Finish the embedded sentences below.***

1. Would you mind telling me ______________________________
   ______________________________?
2. I'm not sure ______________________________
   ______________________________?
3. Do you remember ______________________________
   ______________________________?

Speaking Skill: Active Listening

Active Listening is the ability to: (1) completely focus on the speaker's words, (2) understand their meaning and intent and (3) respond thoughtfully. You can listen actively by using these strategies:

Verbal	Nonverbal
- Ask specific, open-ended questions - Use short, verbal affirmations *"Ah", "Uh-huh", "I see", "Okay",* - Recall previously shared info - Share similar experiences - Paraphrase: *"So you're saying that..."*	- Make occasional eye contact - Smile - Nod

Avoiding certain behaviorsis also an important part of active listening.
Try to avoid distracted body language (fidgeting, looking away), interrupting others, and checking your phone too often. Instead, try to focus on the speaker's words without thinking about what you'll say next.

Tip: Enter a conversation with a "listen first" mindset.

A. Practice. ***Read the following conversation. Using active listening skills, substitute the underlined sentences for better ones.***

Brian	Hey, man. I'm having a really hard time right now. Do you mind listening and giving me some advice?	______________________ ______________________ ______________________
Jason	Yeah, sure. Did you see Hyun's post on Instagram? He went to Busan again. He's crazy...	______________________ ______________________ ______________________
Brian	No, but I need some advice about my relationship.	______________________ ______________________ ______________________
Jason	Yeah, hang on. I need to call my girlfriend. We're going drinking. You can join, right?	______________________ ______________________ ______________________

B. More Practice. ***In your team, use open-ended questions to have a conversation. Start with "How are you these days?"then ask only questions to keep the conversation going as long as possible.***

Wrap-Up

A. Write & Talk. ***Practice asking and answering the questions below to have a conversation with a partner or group.***

1. What job do you want to do in the future? Is it a modern job or has it existed for a long time?

   ____

   ____

2. Is the job you want to do in the future related to the Internet? How so?

   ____

   ____

3. Do you think your future job will exist in 100 years?

   ____

   ____

4. If you did not have to worry about things like money or training, what job would you like to do in the future?

   ____

   ____

5. Do you think automation is a problem now? What about in the future?

   ____

   ____

B. Quiz. ***Take the quiz below to see how well you understood the unit.***

1. Ji-eun is studying French, but she always gets nervous during __________ with native speakers because they talk so fast and it's difficult to __________ with what they're saying.

   a. interactions, keep up
   c. ethical, pop up
   b. automation, keep up
   d. Emerging, represent

2. Jobs have always changed over time to respond to the needs of society, but the jobs today are changing quickly thanks to __________ and __________. (Select two.)

a. the Internet
b. new skills
c. data
d. automation

3. I don't think Kenan __________ with his family when he visits home next week. He said they had an argument.

a. stays
b. Is not staying
c. will be staying
d. won't be staying

4. The drastic increase in popularity of Korean culture abroad __________ more people than ever interested in learning Korean and consuming Korean media.

a. as a result
b. has resulted in
c. best of both worlds
d. due to

5. Listening is an important part of having a conversation.

a. True
b. False

Notes. ***Use the space below to take notes on this unit.***

Unit 12

The Future, Education, and You

In this Unit...

Vocabulary	Grammar
up to you, in charge of, advent, trial and error, plethora, step-by-step, vast, abundant	Acronyms and Portmanteau
Reading Topic	**Speaking Skill**
Lifelong Learning	English for Social Media

Building Communication
from here on out, make the most of it, (stay/keep) on one's toes

Preview

A. Conversation. *Read the text message exchange below.*

Omg!

What?

Did u c that video
Shawn posted on IG?

Yeah, he's getting srsly
good at making videos

idk how he learned to
make that. I wanna learn
to do smth cool like that too

You can, y'know

??? how?

u could study

But I don't have time

Shawn's really busy too.
He works a full time job like us,
but he finds the time to learn

tbh learning smth new is rly difficult

It is, but if u r motivated,
then u can do it

ur right. thnx for the advice

Np. So what r u
going to try learning?

idk yet but i will find smth

B. Warm-up. *Write four subjects or topics you would like to learn in your own time.*

When you graduate university, will you continue to study?

When you have your own time, what would you like to learn?

1. ______________________ 3. ______________________
2. ______________________ 4. ______________________

C. Write & Discuss. *Write 2-3 sentences about one of the topics above that you would like. What makes you interested in that topic?*

____

____

____

Vocabulary Focus

A. Definition Matching. *Write the letter next to the correct word.*

_______	1. up to you	A. beginning or arrival
_______	2. in charge of	B. your choice or responsibility
_______	3. advent	C. a very large amount
_______	4. trial and error	D. plenty of, more than enough
_______	5. plethora	E. having control or responsibility for
_______	6. step-by-step	F. very big in size, amount, or degree
_______	7. vast	G. trying different methods to find the best
_______	8. abundant	H. making slow, careful progress

B. Fill in the Blanks. *Write the correct vocabulary word from above.*

1. If you want to improve your English after university, it's ______________. No one will force you to continue your education.
2. I never properly learned how to make a website. I just decided to try and I learned through ________________.
3. In my dream, I sat on top of a waterfall that looked over a __________ jungle.
4. My brother works at a technology company. But he's not an engineer or anything, he's ________________ security.
5. Food is ________________ in most developed countries. However, many people around the world lack access to food and proper nutrition.
6. Many countries have festivals to celebrate the end of winter and the ________________ of spring.
7. There are a ________________ of reasons why I don't shop at the department store supermarket. Most of all, it's too expensive.
8. If you're new to baking, it's a good idea to follow each recipe ________.

The Future, Education, and You

Congratulations! Why? Because, believe it or not, you're almost finished with your formal education. *In fact*, this might be the last English class you ever take. *From here on out*, you're on your own. When you finish college, will you keep studying English? Will you continue reading new books and learning new skills? While the opportunities for self-education and self-development are bigger than ever before, your future progress is ultimately up to you and how much you want it. What does your future hold?

As your formal education ends, you'll be in charge of your education. But how do people learn outside of school? Before the advent of the Internet, the world was much less connected. There was no online shopping, Instagram, or YouTube. If you wanted to learn a new skill, you had to take a class, find someone who knew how to do it, or buy a book from an expert and experiment through trial and error. While these are still great ways to learn, we now have access to a plethora of experts, amateurs, and everything in between. There's more knowledge than our ancestors could ever imagine! Perhaps you want to learn about French fashion, how to sail a boat, or how to master a computer game. You can get detailed, step-by-step instructions from the best people in the world. However, there is still one thing that we cannot find online.

What is it? Motivation. Despite having access to a vast amount of knowledge, many of us don't *make the most of* it. But if you make a choice to continue your self-development, you'll find that anything is possible. You can learn the in-and-outs of French fashion, how to captain a sailboat, or become a master of that game. You can write a book, build a computer, or become a chef. Connect with others who share your passions, learn together, and get feedback. This will keep you *on your toes*.

Although your formal education may be coming to a close, that doesn't mean that you have to stop learning. We live in a time of abundant information, but we still require the key ingredient: motivation. Your future is in your hands. Go get 'em!

Comprehension Check

A. Summary. ***Fill each blank with information from the text.***

Is this your last English class? It just might be. After you graduate from college, you will have to decide whether you will continue to study or not. There are so many opportunities for self-education and ________________, but you have to want it. Before the ________________ of the Internet, people who wanted to acquire new skills had to take ________________, buy a book or experiment themselves. Our ________________ never dreamed of this much knowledge! However, there is one essential thing that we cannot find online: ________________ . That part must come from inside you. But when you make that choice, you'll find that you can accomplish anything.

B. True/False. ***If the sentence is false, correct it to make it true.***

1. Opportunities for self-education are quite low. (T/F)
2. We have access to an unprecedented amount of knowledge. (T/F)
3. Motivation can be found online. (T/F)
4. People often end up taking the path of least resistance. (T/F)
5. Your future education choices are up to you. (T/F)

C. Short Answer. ***Answer each question with information from the text.***

1. What are some ways that people had to learn new things in the past?

   ____

   ____

2. According to the text, what will keep you on your toes?

   ____

   ____

Building Communication

A. Learn. *Look at the phrases below to learn how to use them.*

1. from here on out - from now on

   You're an adult now. From here on out, you need to be responsible for yourself.

2. make the most (best) of - enjoy or use as much as possible

   Even though it's raining, we should still make the best of our beach vacation.

3. (stay/keep) on one's toes - alert and ready for anything

   A: *It's dark so let's be careful walking home.*

   B: *Yeah. We should stay on our toes.*

B. Practice. *Complete the sentences with the phrases from above.*

1. Well, if we can't travel overseas, we can still ______________________ our vacation by going to Jeju!
2. ______________________, we're gonna save money. So we should avoid buying snacks at the convenience store.
3. If you want to get a good job, timing is important. So always ______________________ and be ready for an interview at any time.

C. More Practice. *Make sentences using the phrases above.*

1. from here on out

   ____

2. make the most (best) of ~

   ____

3. stay (keep) on one's toes

   ____

Grammar: Acronyms and Portmanteau

Languages have ways to shorten words or phrases to be more efficient or create new words.

Acronym

An *acronym* is a word made using the first letter (or first few letters) of a longer name/phrase. They are pronounced like normal a word.

→ An *initialism* is a type of acronym that is made of only the first letters of several words in a phrase.

Daily Life		*Online**	
PIN	→ personal identification number	TBH	→ to be honest?
OTC	→ over the counter	NVM	→ never mind
ATM	→ automated teller machine	RN	→ right now?
		IDK	→ I don't know

Portmanteau

A *portmanteau* is a word made by mixing parts of several words together.

Daily Life		*Online*	
Spam	→ spiced + ham	WiFi	→ wireless + fidelity
bromance	→ brother + romance	pixel	→ picture + element
hangry	→ hungry + angry	vlog	→ video + blog
Konglish	→ Korean + English	widget	→ window + gadget

A. Practice. ***Complete the sentences below with the correct acronym or portmanteau.***

1. You need to bring your __________ card that has information like your name, age, etc. to prove who you are.
2. A: Can you check where we are going? I think we're lost. B: I'm trying but I can't get a __________ signal on my phone.
3. When I'm sick, I just go to the pharmacy and pick up __________ medicine because getting a prescription is annoying.
4. __________, that cake she made wasn't very good, but I can't tell her that.

Speaking Skill: English for Social Media

On the Internet, English is used both formally (news, education, work) and informally (chatting, entertainment). Social media (SNS) is filled with informal English. You might also see symbols and text emoticons.

Internet English	Meaning	Internet English	Meaning
lol	laugh out loud	np	no problem
brb	be right back	ttyl	talk to you later
hmu	hit me up (contact me)	srsly	seriously
lmk	let me know	smth	something
idk	I don't know	plz	please
tbh	to be honest	thx	thanks
gonna + (v.)	going to + (v.)	wanna	want to
:/	unsure	XD	funny, laughing

A. Practice. ***Rewrite the following conversation using abbreviations.***

Minhee	Jason. Can you let me know something, please?	____________________ ____________________
Jason	Maybe. I don't know. What is it?	____________________ ____________________
Minhee	To be honest, I'm not sure what to study for the test.	____________________ ____________________
Jason	Oh, no problem. It's going to be seriously easy.	____________________ ____________________
Minhee	I want to study this weekend.	____________________ ____________________
Jason	No problem. I'll contact you later.	____________________ ____________________
Minhee	Thanks! Talk to you later.	____________________ ____________________

B. More Practice. ***Search online for 3 more unique online slang or abbreviations. Write them below.***

1. ____________________, 2. ____________________, 3. ____________________

Wrap-Up

A. Write & Talk. ***Practice asking and answering the questions below to have a conversation with a partner or group.***

1. Will you continue studying English after university? Why or why not?

____

____

2. What topics do you want to study when you have your own time?

____

____

3. If you could get step-by-step instructions from anyone in the world about a topic or skill, who would it be and which topic or skill?

____

____

4. What do you do when you don't feel motivated?

____

____

5. What is one important skill you have learned outside of school?

____

____

B. Quiz. ***Take the quiz below to see how well you understood the unit.***

1. Learning something new takes time, but if you do it __________ and learn through __________, then you will be a master in no time!

   a. vast, plethora
   b. up to you, abundant
   c. step-by-step, trial and error
   d. trial and error, advent

2. Many people think their education stops after they finish school, but that's not true. People want to learn things but usually lack __________ to actually study.

   a. motivation
   b. education
   c. self-development
   d. skills

3. Lee was always looking for new opportunities to make money so he always __________ in case something popped up.

a. believed it or not
b. made the most of it
c. stayed on his toes
d. from here on out

4. Did you hear Hilda play the piano? She's amazing! She told me she __________ since she was six. No wonder she's so good.

a. played
b. has been playing
c. is playing
d. was playing

5. Which word best completes the conversation below? A: Hey! Where are you going? We aren't finished talking. B: I know. I'll __________. I need to go to the bathroom really quickly. We can finish talking when I return.

a. lyk
b. brb
c. ttyl
d. plz

Notes. ***Use the space below to take notes on this unit.***

References

Montasser Mohamed. (2013). Developing an English language textbook evaluative checklist. *Journal of Research & Method in Education. 1*(3), P 55-70.

Myeong-Hee Seong & Daniel Cuffey. (2021). *Trending Topics*. 서울: 지식인

Myeong-Hee Seong & Daniel Cuffey, Erika Choe & Chase Karcher. (2019). *The Big Picture*. 서울: 지식인.

Wuttisrisiriporn, Niwat & Usaha, Sinluck. (2019). The development of a localized ELT textbook evaluation checklist: A case study from Thailand. *THAITESOL, 32*(2), p46-64.

Sources

[Unit 1]

- Title Picture: https://pixabay.com/photos/girl-laptop-school-supplies-student-5662435/
- NCES Report: https://nces.ed.gov/pubs2019/2019021REV.pdf
- Absentee issue: https://www.nytimes.com/2020/04/06/us/coronavirus-schools-attendance-absent.html
- Disadvantages of eLearning: https://elearningindustry.com/5-common-problems-faced-by-students-in-elearning-overcome
- Prestigious universities offer online courses: https://www.lifehack.org/articles/money/25-killer-sites-for-free-online-education.html
- Advantages of eLearning: https://elearningindustry.com/5-advantages-of-online-learning-education-without-leaving-home

[Unit 2]

- Title Picture: https://pixabay.com/illustrations/climate-change-global-warming-2254711/

- Effects of Climate Change: https://climate.nasa.gov/effects/
- United States, Increasing Number of Climate Change Events: https://www.climate.gov/news-features/blogs/beyond-data/2010-2019-landmark-decade-us-billion-dollar-weather-and-climate
- Climate Change Trends Reported Around the World: https://news.un.org/en/story/2020/10/1075142
- Causes of Climate Change: https://climate.nasa.gov/causes/
- Currently Fighting Climate Change:
  https://www.nationalgeographic.com/environment/global-warming/global-warming-solutions/
  https://www.unenvironment.org/resources/emissions-gap-report-2018
  https://time.com/person-of-the-year-2019-greta-thunberg/
- How We Can Help: https://www.wwf.org.uk/thingsyoucando

[Unit 3]

- Title Picture: https://pixabay.com/photos/travel-airport-boarding-pass-5219496/
- On Human Migration: https://www.sciencedirect.com/science/article/pii/S0960982218311217
- Korea Outbound Travel Statistics: https://www.statista.com/statistics/1141893/south-korea-outbound-tourist-departures/
- Korea Travel and Tourism: https://en.wikipedia.org/wiki/Tourism_in_South_Korea

[Unit 4]

- Title Picture: https://pixabay.com/photos/create-craft-peaceful-work-865017/
- History of teleworking: https://www.alliedtelecom.net/the-history-of-telecommuting/
- How the pandemic has (and hasn't) changed the way Americans work (Pew Research): https://www.pewresearch.org/social-trends/2020/12/09/how-the-coronavirus-outbreak-has-and-hasnt-changed-the-way-americans-work/#looking-ahead-a-

majority-of-those-who-say-their-job-can-be-done-from-home-say-theyd-like-to-telework-all-or-most-of-the-time-post-pandemic

[Unit 5]

- Title Picture:
  https://cdn.pixabay.com/photo/2017/10/10/21/49/youtuber-2838945_960_720.jpg
- Vacation Time Utilization/Vacation Deprivation:
  https://www.cepr.net/documents/publications/no-vacation-update-2013-05.pdf
  https://www.weforum.org/agenda/2018/08/people-in-these-countries-get-the-most-paid-vacation-days/
  https://viewfinder.expedia.com/vacation-deprivation/
- Korean Labor Law:
  https://www.koreanlaborlaw.com/annual-leave-based-on-the-korean-labor-law/
- Signs of burnout:
  https://www.mayoclinic.org/healthy-lifestyle/adult-health/in-depth/burnout/art-20046642

[Unit 6]

- Title Picture:
  https://pixabay.com/photos/city-people-underground-metro-1940691/
- US statistic:
  https://www.epa.gov/transportation-air-pollution-and-climate-change/carbon-pollution-transportation
- Australia's statistics:
  https://mozo.com.au/insurance/car-insurance/articles/the-costs-and-environmental-impact-of-transport-in-2021
- Places with cheap taxis:
  https://www.smartertravel.com/countries-cheap-taxi-rides/

[Unit 7]

- Title Picture:
  https://pixabay.com/photos/angry-shouting-man-shout-scream-6319463/
- On Eustress:

https://www.healthline.com/health/eustress

- Adolescent Stress in Korea:
  https://www.ncbi.nlm.nih.gov/pmc/articles/PMC6210583/
- Stress and Health:
  https://www.webmd.com/balance/stress-management/effects-of-stress-on-your-body
- Managing Stress:
  https://www.webmd.com/balance/guide/tips-to-control-stress

[Unit 8]

- Title Picture:
  https://pixabay.com/photos/people-men-discuss-paper-pen-2561336/
- Language and Culture:
  https://www.britannica.com/topic/language/Language-and-culture
- Managing Intercultural Conflict:
  https://www.universalclass.com/articles/business/intercultural-communication/how-to-manage-intercultural-conflicts.htm

[Unit 9]

- Title Picture:
  https://pixabay.com/photos/money-coin-investment-business-2724241/
- Financial Education:
  https://www.investopedia.com/articles/investing/100615/why-financial-literacy-and-education-so-important.asp
- Compound Interest:
  https://www.investopedia.com/terms/c/compoundinterest.asp
- Good Financial Habits:
  https://bfsfcu.org/post/build_good_financial_habits.html?psrc=50

[Unit 10]

- Title Picture:
  https://pixabay.com/photos/crafts-ceramics-pottery-porcelain-5276736/
- History of Leisure:

https://www.etymonline.com/word/leisure
https://en.wikipedia.org/wiki/Leisure

[Unit 11]

- Title Picture:
  https://pixabay.com/photos/solar-panels-placement-green-energy-943999/
- Reasons for job changes:
  https://www.weforum.org/reports/the-future-of-jobs-report-2020/digest

[Unit 12]

- Title Picture:
  https://cdn.pixabay.com/photo/2016/09/26/04/03/graduation-1695185_960_720.jpg

Looking Forward